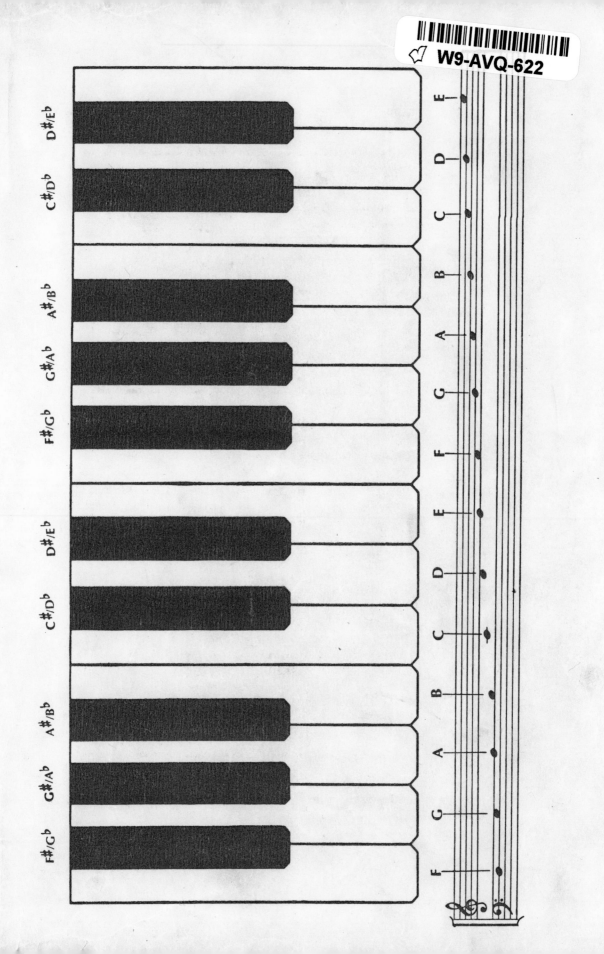
W9-AVQ-622

# World of Music

Jane Beethoven • Jennifer Davidson
Catherine Nadon-Gabrion
**Authors**

Carmino Ravosa • Phyllis Weikart
Theme Musical  Movement

Darrell Bledsoe
Producer, Vocal Recordings

## Silver Burdett & Ginn
Morristown, NJ • Needham, MA
Atlanta, GA • Cincinnati, OH • Dallas, TX • Menlo Park, CA • Northfield, IL

© 1988 Silver, Burdett & Ginn Inc. All rights reserved. Printed in the United States of America. Published simultaneously in Canada. This publication, or parts thereof, may not be reproduced in any form by photographic, electrostatic, mechanical, or any other method, for any use, including information storage and retrieval, without written permission from the publisher.
ISBN 0-382-07046-1

# Contents

## Sharing Music 138

## Sing and Celebrate 184

## Reference Bank 222

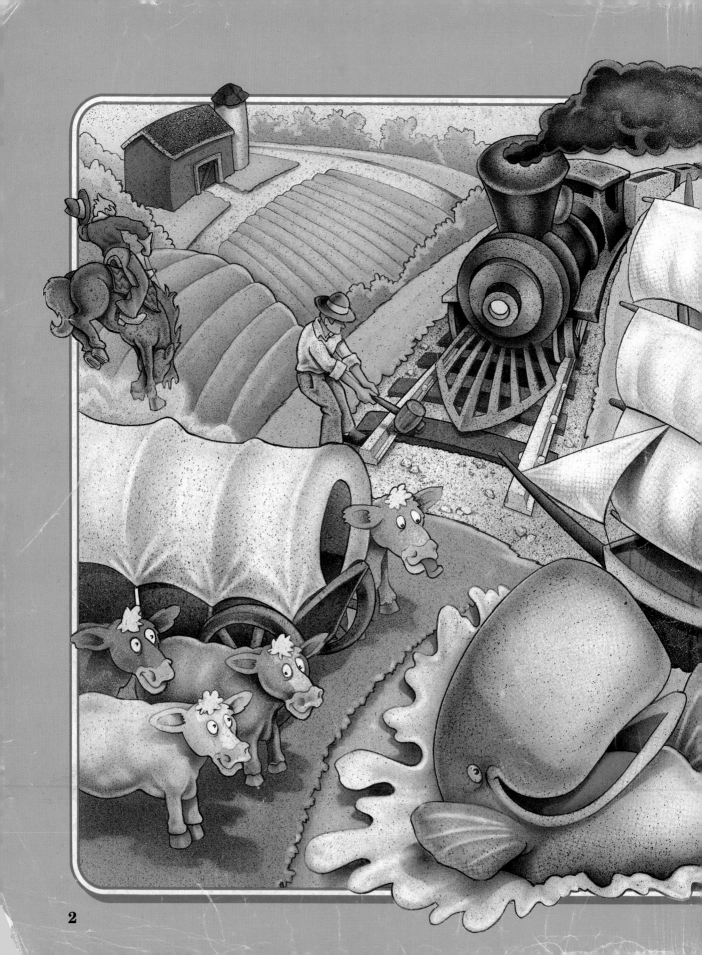

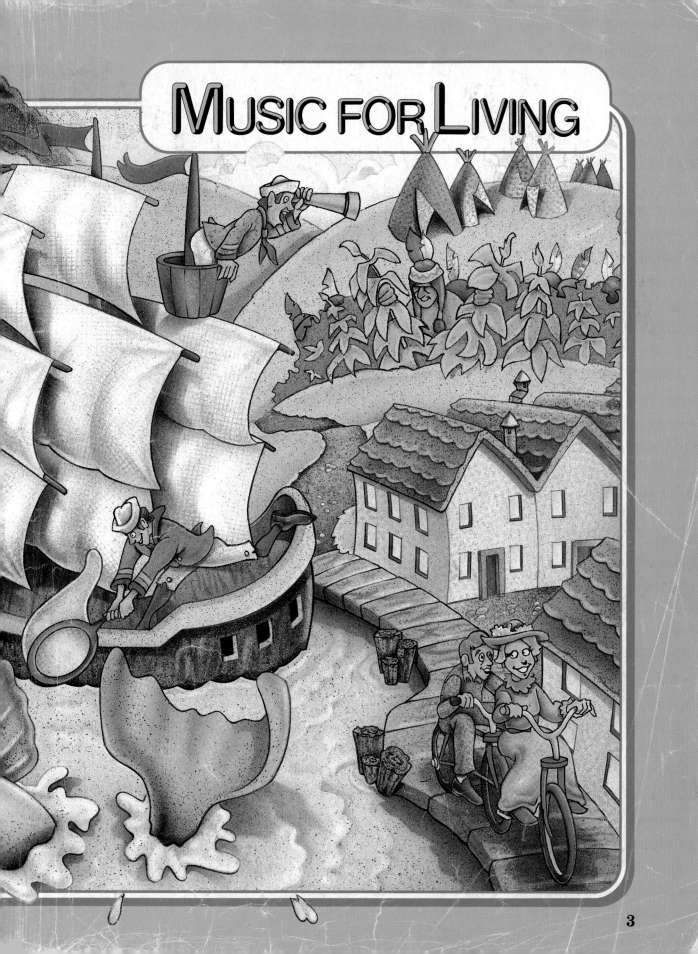

# MUSIC FOR LIVING

# Sing About Your Land

If you made up a song about your land, what are some of the things you might sing about?

## This Land Is Your Land

Words and Music by Woody Guthrie

REFRAIN

This land is your land, ___ This land is my land ___
From Cal - i - for - nia ___ to the New York is - land; ___
From the red-wood for - est ___ to the Gulf Stream wa - ters; ___
This land was made for you and me. ___

VERSE

1. As I was walk - ing ___ that rib-bon of high - way, ___
I saw a - bove me ___ that end - less sky - way. ___

Words and Music by Woody Guthrie TRO—© Copyright 1956 (renewed 1984), 1958 (renewed 1986) and 1970 Ludlow Music, Inc., New York, N.Y. Used by permission.

I saw be - low me _____ that gold - en val - ley, _____

This land was made for you and me. _____

*D.C. al Fine*

2. I've roamed and rambled and I followed my footsteps
   To the sparkling sands of her diamond deserts,
   And all around me a voice was sounding,
   "This land was made for you and me." *Refrain*

3. When the sun comes shining and I was strolling
   And the wheatfields waving and the dust clouds rolling,
   As the fog was lifting a voice was chanting,
   "This land was made for you and me." *Refrain*

# Party in the Barn

Long ago, people harvested their crops by hand. When the hard work of the summer was done, the farmers and their families had a party in the barn. "Shuckin' of the Corn" was one of the songs they sang.

## Shuckin' of the Corn

Folk Song from Tennessee

1. I have a ship on the o - cean, _____
2. The wind blows cold in ____ Cai - ro, _____

All lined with sil - ver and gold. _____
The sun re - fus - es to shine. _____

Be - fore I'd see my true love suf - fer,
Be - fore I'd see my true love suf - fer,

That ship should be an - chored and sold. _____
I'd work all the sum - mer time. _____

**REFRAIN**

I'm a - go - ing to the shuck - in' of the corn, _____

Flora L. McDowell from MEMORY MELODIES

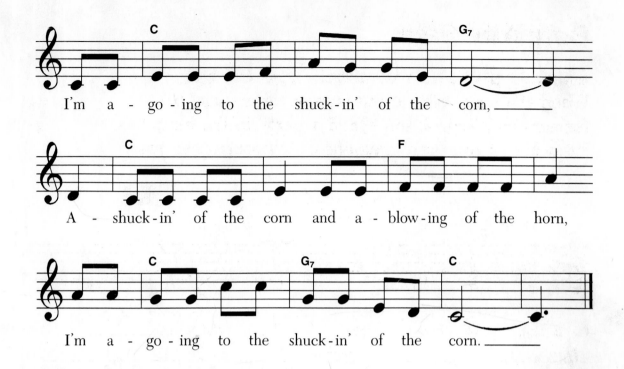

I'm a - go - ing to the shuck-in' of the corn, _____

A - shuck-in' of the corn and a - blow-ing of the horn,

I'm a - go - ing to the shuck-in' of the corn. _____

## Play a Pattern

Use sandblocks to play the steady beat. Tap the tambourine on the first beat of every measure.

Sandblocks

Tambourine

# Down on the Farm

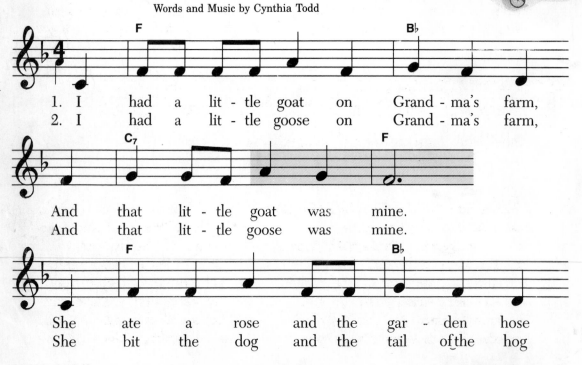

Did you ever hear of
a goat who ate a rose?
This song tells about the goat,
as well as three other animals.

## Grandma's Farm

Words and Music by Cynthia Todd

1. I had a lit - tle goat on Grand - ma's farm,
2. I had a lit - tle goose on Grand - ma's farm,

And that lit - tle goat was mine.
And that lit - tle goose was mine.

She ate a rose and the gar - den hose
She bit the dog and the tail of the hog

© 1985 Cynthia Todd

And the sheets on Grand - ma's line.
And she hid be - hind the vine.

And the sheets on Grand - ma's line,
And she hid be - hind the vine,

And the sheets on Grand - ma's line,
And she hid be - hind the vine,

She ate a rose and the gar - den hose
She bit the dog and the tail of the hog

And the sheets on Grand - ma's line.
And she hid be - hind the vine.

3. I had a little pig on Grandma's farm,
   And that little pig was mine.
   She snorted once and snorted twice
   And she slept underneath the pine.
   And she slept underneath the pine,
   And she slept underneath the pine.
   She snorted once and snorted twice
   And she slept underneath the pine.

4. I had a little cow on Grandma's farm,
   And that little cow was mine.
   She ate all day and ran away,
   Said Grandma, "It's a crime."
   Said Grandma, "It's a crime."
   Said Grandma, "It's a crime."
   She ate all day and ran away,
   Said Grandma, "It's a crime."

# A Good Place to Be

Many people who came to the
United States from other countries
came here to start a better life.
Some farmers from Norway
thought Oleana would be a
good place to settle. The words
of this song will tell you why.

## Oleana

Norwegian Emigrant Song     English Words by Polly Budd

1. O - le - an - a,  O - le - an - a,  Far a - cross the deep blue sea,
**REFRAIN:** O - le, O - le - an - a, ___ O - le, O - le - an - a,

O - le - an - a,  O - le - an - a,  That is where I'd like to be.
O - le, O - le, O - le, O - le,  O - le, O - le - an - a.

2. Oleana, that's the place,
   That is where I'll settle down;
   It's a place where land is free
   And money trees grow all around.

3. Corn and wheat grow to the sky,
   All according to the plan;
   Sheep and cows do all the work
   And fish jump in the frying pan.

4. There the crops just plant themselves,
   There the sun shines night and day;
   Harvest time comes once a month,
   But farmers only sing and play.

5. Ole Bull will play for us,
   Play upon his violin;
   And we'll sing and dance together,
   Happier than we've ever been.

# Add Instruments

Here are three patterns you can use to accompany "Oleana." Which pattern will you choose?

# Mother Corn

It was the American Indians who taught the early settlers how to raise corn.

Pawnee Indians spoke of corn as *Atira,* meaning "mother." *H* means "breath of life."

## H'Atira

Pawnee Corn Song

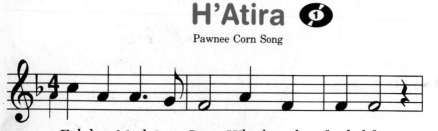

Fol - low Moth - er  Corn, Who breathes forth life.

H'A - ti - ra,    H'A - ti - ra,    H'A - ti - ra,    A - ti - ra,

H'A - ti - ra,    A - ti - ra,    H'A - ti - ra,    A - ti - ra,

A - ti - ra,    H'A - ti - ra,    A - ti - ra.

# Drum and Rattle

Play the drum and rattle patterns as an introduction.
You can also use the patterns to accompany the song.

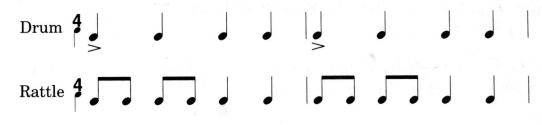

Drum

Rattle

## Far as Man Can See

Far as man can see,
  Comes the rain,
  Comes the rain with me.

From the Rain-Mount,
Rain-Mount far away,
  Comes the rain,
  Comes the rain with me.

O'er the corn,
O'er the corn, tall corn,
  Comes the rain,
  Comes the rain with me.

'Mid the lightnings,
'Mid the lightning zigzag,
'Mid the lightning flashing,
  Comes the rain,
  Comes the rain with me.

Far as man can see
  Comes the rain,
  Comes the rain with me.

From *Song of the Rain-Chant*

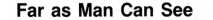

# A Happy Song

People often sing and dance when they are happy.
This Navaho Indian song was sung at feasts and
on other joyous occasions.

When you sing the song, let your voice show
that the song is a happy song.

## Navaho Happy Song

Navaho Indian Song

Hi yo, hi yo, ip si ni yah, hi yo,

Hi yo ip si ni — yah, hi — yo, Hi yo ip si

ni yah, hi — yo, Hi yo ip si ni yah,

*(Last time only)*

Ip si ni yah!

Courtesy of Janet Tobitt from THE DITTY BAG.

In this recording you will hear members of the
Navaho tribe singing one of their songs.

*Navaho Night Chant* . . . . . . American Indian

14

# Drum and Rattle Accompaniment

Here are two parts for instruments. Which part will you play to accompany the singing?

## I Walk with Beauty

In beauty happily I walk.
With beauty before me, I walk.
With beauty behind me, I walk.
With beauty below me, I walk.
With beauty above me, I walk.
With beauty all around me, I walk.

It is finished again in beauty,
It is finished in beauty,
It is finished in beauty,
It is finished in beauty.

From *The Night Chant, A Navaho Ceremony*

# Making Instruments

American Indians accompany their songs and dances by playing instruments. You can make your own instruments and play accompaniments for songs in your book.

## Drums

A long time ago, people in certain tribes made a drum by turning a basket upside down on the ground. They would beat the drum with their hands or with a stick. You can make your own drum from containers that you might find at home: cereal boxes, hat boxes, and round ice-cream cartons.

Drums can also be made from small wooden barrels or wooden salad bowls. Drumheads may be made by stretching old inner tubes or heavy fabric over the top of the drum body.

To make a tom-tom, you will need a container that is open at both ends. A drumhead must be attached at each end. The two heads may be laced together with leather strips or heavy shoelaces.

You may play a drum with your hands or with a hard or soft drumstick. To make a soft drumstick, tie a clump of absorbent cotton around the end of a stick.

## Shakers

You can make a shaking rattling instrument by putting small objects into any kind of container. The rattling objects can be pebbles, wooden beads, dried beans, or grains of rice.

Rain rattles may be made by fastening small shells or tiny pieces of metal to a stick. The small objects will jingle when the stick is shaken.

# A Home Out-of-Doors

If you traveled around the world, you would see all kinds of homes. This song tells about a home out-of-doors.

## Home on the Range

American Cowboy Song

1. Oh, give me a home where the buf - fa - lo roam,
2. How of - ten at night when the heav - ens are bright

Where the deer and the an - te - lope play, _____
With the lights from the glit - ter - ing stars, _____

Where sel - dom is heard a dis - cour - ag - ing word,
Have I stood there a - mazed and _____ asked as I gazed,

And the skies are not cloud - y all day. _____
If their glo - ry ex - ceeds that of ours. _____

REFRAIN

Home, home on the range, _____

18

Where the deer and the an - te - lope play, _____

Where sel - dom is heard a dis - cour - ag - ing word,

And the skies are not cloud - y all day. _____

## Open Range

Prairie goes to the mountain,
   Mountain goes to the sky.
The sky sweeps across to the distant hills
And here, in the middle,
   Am I.

Hills crowd down to the river,
   River runs by the tree.
Tree throws its shadow on sunburnt grass
And here, in the shadow,
   Is me.

Shadows creep up the mountain,
   Mountain goes black on the sky,
The sky bursts out with a million stars
And here, by the campfire,
   Am I.

*Kathryn and Byron Jackson*

## Easy Rider

This song is about someone who went west to become a cowhand. Listen to the recording to find out more about this fellow.

# My Home's in Montana

American Cowboy Song    Words Adapted by W. S. Williams

1. My home's in Mon - tan - a, I left In - di - an - a
2. I learned how to las - so Way down in El Pa - so,

To start a new life Far a - way in the West;
I've fol - lowed the cat - tle Wher - ev - er they roam;

My skin's rough as leath - er, Made tough by the weath - er;
I'm wear - y of stray - ing, Right here I'll be stay - ing,

The wind and the sun Of the land I love best.
I'll wan - der no more For Mon - tan - a's my home.

20

## Play a Part

Choose one of these patterns to accompany "My Home's in Montana." Which pattern will you choose? Play it all through the song.

# A Cowhand's Lullaby

Motherless calves are called *dogies*. The cowhand sings to the dogies to quiet them at night. If you were a cowhand, how would you use your voice to quiet the dogies?

# Night Herding Song 1

American Cowboy Song

1. Oh, slow up, do - gies, quit rov - ing a - round,

You have wan - dered and tram - pled all o - ver the ground;

Oh, graze a - long, do - gies, and feed kind - a slow,

And don't for - ev - er be on the go.

Oh, move slow, do - gies, move slow, _____

Hi - oo, hi - oo, _____ hi - oo! _____

2. I've circle herded and night herded too,
But to keep you together, that's what I can't do;
My horse is leg weary, and I'm awful tired,
But if you get away, I am sure to get fired.
Bunch up, little dogies, bunch up,
Hi-oo, hi-oo, hi-oo!

3. Oh, lie still, dogies, since you have lain down,
Stretch away out on the big open ground;
Snore loud, little dogies, and drown the wild sound,
That will all go away when the day rolls round.
Lie still, little dogies, lie still.
Hi-oo, hi-oo, hi-oo!

## Bell Part

Use the bells to play the *Hi-oo* parts at
the end of each verse.

The letters under the bell part will tell
you which bells you will need.

F   A       G

# Under the Big Top

Aaron Copland, a famous American composer, wrote the music for a movie called *The Red Pony*. The movie is about a ten-year-old boy named Jody, who received a red pony as a gift from his father. Jody loved his pony and often dreamed about the wonderful things they could do together. In one of his dreams, Jody was a ringmaster at a circus, putting his pony through his act.

Here is the music Copland wrote for Jody's imaginary day at the circus. Does the music sound like circus music to you?

LISTENING SKILLS 1    "Circus Music" from *The Red Pony* . . Copland

# Listening for the Theme

Here is a melody, or theme, that Copland used in his "Circus Music." Do you hear the theme in section A or in section B?

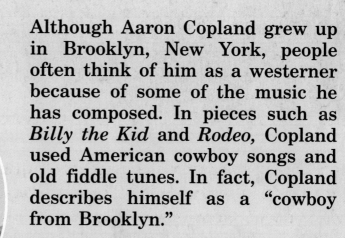

Although Aaron Copland grew up in Brooklyn, New York, people often think of him as a westerner because of some of the music he has composed. In pieces such as *Billy the Kid* and *Rodeo,* Copland used American cowboy songs and old fiddle tunes. In fact, Copland describes himself as a "cowboy from Brooklyn."

In addition to *The Red Pony,* Copland has written music for several other movies. He has composed music for the stage and concert hall as well. Aaron Copland is one of America's finest composers. His music is heard and loved by audiences all over the world.

Aaron Copland
(1900–    )

# A Sailor's Work Song

Pretend that you are a sailor on board a clipper ship. Swab the deck or hoist the sails in time to the music of this old sea shantey.

## Johnny Come to Hilo

Sea Shantey

Oh, a poor old — man came a - rid - ing — by,
Says I "Old man, your — horse will die."
Oh, John - ny, come to Hi - lo, oh, poor old man.
Oh, wake her, oh, shake her;
Oh, swing that girl with the blue dress on.
Oh, John - ny, come to Hi - lo, Oh, poor old man.

## Clipper Ships and Captains

There was a time before our time,
It will not come again,
When the best ships still were wooden ships,
But the men were iron men.

The skippers with the little beards
And the New England drawl,
Who knew Hong Kong and Marblehead
And the Pole Star over all.

Stately as churches, swift as gulls,
They trod the oceans, then;
No man has seen such ships before
And none will see again.

*Rosemary and Stephen Vincent Benet*

# A Song that Tells a Story

Many years ago, whaling ships sailed out of Massachusetts. This is a song that the sailors sang to amuse themselves aboard ship.

## Blow, Ye Winds

American Folk Song

1. 'Tis ad-ver-tised in Bos-ton, New York, and Buf-fa-lo,
2. They send you to New Bed-ford, that fa-mous whal-ing port,

Five hun-dred brave A-mer-i-cans, a-whal-ing for to go.
And give you to some land sharks to board and fit you out.

**REFRAIN**

Sing-ing, "Blow, ye winds in the morn-ing, And blow, ye winds, high-O!

Clear a-way your run-ning gear, And blow, ye winds, high-O!"

3. They tell you of the clipper ships
   a-going in and out,
   And say you'll take five hundred sperm
   before you're six months out.

4. It's now we're out to sea, my boys,
   the wind begins to blow,
   One half the watch is sick on deck
   and the other half below.

From SONGS OF AMERICAN SAILORMEN by Joanna C. Colcord. By permission of W. W. Norton & Co., Inc. © 1938 Copyright renewed 1966 by the Boone County State Bank, Lebanon, Indiana, Executor of the estate of the author.

5. The skipper's on the quarter-deck
     a-squinting at the sails,
   When up aloft the look-out sights
     a school of whales.

6. "Now clear away the boats, my boys,
     and after him we'll trail,
   But if you get too near to him,
     he'll kick you with his tail!"

7. Now we've got him turned up,
     we tow him alongside;
   We over with our blubber hooks
     and rob him of his hide.

8. Next comes the stowing down, my boys,
     'twill take both night and day,
   And you'll all have fifty cents apiece
     when you collect your pay.

# Fisherman's Song

Not long after America was discovered, fishing villages appeared along the rugged coast of Newfoundland. Here is a song that the fishermen sang when the long day's work was done.

As you listen to the song, pat your knees in time to the music.

## I'se the B'y

Folk Song from Newfoundland    New Words and New Music Adaptation by Oscar Brand

1. I'se the b'y that builds the boat, I'se the b'y that sails her.

I'se the b'y that catch-es the fish And brings them home to Li - za.

**REFRAIN**

Swing your part-ner, Sal - ly Tib-ble, Swing your part-ner, Sal - ly Brown.

Swing your part-ner, ev - 'ry-one, All a - round the cir - cle.

2. I took Liza to the dance;
   Faith, but she could travel.
   Ev'ry step that Liza took
   Covered an acre of gravel.

3. Susan White is out of sight,
   Hiding like Jack Horner.
   Choose a lad and take him back,
   Kiss him in the corner.

New words and new music adaptation by Oscar Brand TRO—© Copyright 1957 and renewed 1985 Hollis Music, Inc. New York, N.Y.

## Two Patterns to Play

Can you find these patterns in "I'se the B'y"? Try
playing one of the patterns as the class sings the song.

## An Old Favorite

This old song was a favorite
with the people who worked
on the Erie Canal. Join in on
the refrain as soon as you can.

# Buffalo Gals

American Minstrel Song

1. As I was walk-ing down the street, down the street, down the street,
2. I asked her if she'd stop and talk, stop and talk, stop and talk

A pret-ty girl I chanced to meet, un-der the sil-v'ry moon,
Her feet took up the whole side-walk, there was no __ room for me.

REFRAIN

Oh, Buf-fa-lo gals won't you come out to-night,

come out to-night, come out to-night,

Oh, Buf - fa - lo gals won't you come out to - night

And dance by the light of the moon? ____

3. I asked her if she'd care to walk,
   care to walk, care to walk,
   She said she'd rather stand and talk,
   Oh, she was fair to see. *Refrain*

4. I asked her if she'd care to dance,
   care to dance, care to dance,
   She said that she would take a chance
   And shake a foot with me. *Refrain*

## Autoharp Strum

You can play an accompaniment for "Buffalo Gals" with
only two autoharp chords. Try this strumming pattern.

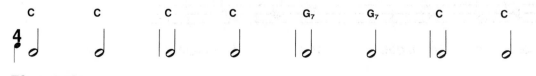

Play 4 times

# Railroad Talk

*Dummy* is the nickname for a small, slow train.
These dummies used to stop at every cow barn to
pick up milk for the city markets.

## The Dummy Line

Folk Song from Southern United States

1. Some folks say that the Dum-my don't run.
   Come and let me tell you what the Dum-my's _ done;
   She left St. Louis at half past one. And she
   rolled in-to Mem-phis at the set-ting of the sun.

2. I got on the Dummy, did-n't have _ my fare,
   Con-duc-tor hol-lered, "What you do-ing _ there?"
   I jumped up and made for the door, And he
   cracked me on the head _ with a two _ by _ four.

**B** REFRAIN

On the Dum-my, _____ on the Dum-my line,

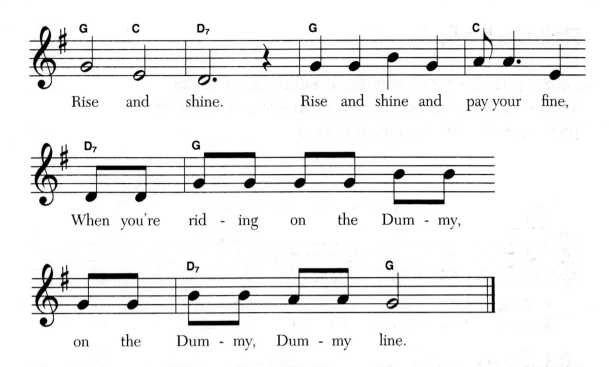

Rise and shine. Rise and shine and pay your fine,

When you're rid - ing on the Dum - my,

on the Dum - my, Dum - my line.

3. I hopped off the Dummy and I lit on the track,
   Dragged my feet and scraped my back.
   I came to life and slung my dogs,
   Looked for sure like I'm on the hog. *Refrain*

4. Some folks say that the Dummy don't run;
   Come and let me tell you what the Dummy's done.
   She left St. Louis at half-past two,
   But I walked to Memphis 'fore the Dummy came through. *Refrain*

Can you find this melody pattern in the song?
Can you sing it? Can you play it on the bells?

Listen for the little train in this recording.

*Train Ride* . . . . . . . . . . . . . . . . . . . . **Anonymous**

# Old American Folk Song

"Old Joe Clark" is as much fun to sing today as it was in the old pioneer days.

There are two different sections in this song. Can you tell where one section ends and the other one begins?

## Old Joe Clark

American Folk Song  Words by Raymond Matthews

1. Old Joe Clark, he built a house, Took him 'bout a week;

He built the floors a-bove his head, The ceil-ings un-der his feet.

**REFRAIN**

Rock-a-rock, Old Joe Clark, Rock-a-rock, I'm gone;

Rock-a-rock, Old Joe Clark, Good-by, Lu-cy Long.

2. Old Joe Clark, he had a dog
   Like none you've ever seen;
   With floppy ears and curly tail,
   And six feet in between. *Refrain*

3. Old Joe Clark, he had a wife,
   Her name was Betty Sue;
   She had two great big brown eyes,
   The other two were blue. *Refrain*

## New Verses for Old Tunes

People have been making up new verses about old
Joe Clark for years. Try singing these verses, then
make up one of your own.

1. Old Joe Clark had a chicken coop
   Eighteen stories high,
   Every chicken in that coop
   Turned into chicken pie.

2. Old Joe Clark he had a cat,
   His tail was ten feet long,
   He wriggled his ears, and laid them flat,
   And sang a mournful song.

## Square-Dance Tune

Like "Old Joe Clark," the song on page 36,
"Pop Goes the Weasel," was a favorite
square-dance tune of the pioneers.

# Pop, Goes the Weasel

American Square Dance Tune

1. All a-round the cob - blers bench, Mon-key chased the wea-sel,
2. The paint-er needs a lad-der and brush, The art - ist needs an ea-sel.

Mon - key thought 'twas all __ in fun, Pop, goes the wea - sel.
Danc-ers need a fid - dler's tune, Pop, goes the wea - sel.

Pen - ny for a spool __ of thread, Pen - ny for a nee - dle,
I've no time to wait or to sigh, No pa-tience to wait till by and by,

That's the way the mon - ey goes, Pop, goes the wea - sel.
Kiss me quick, I'm off, good - bye, Pop, goes the wea - sel.

Listen for square-dance music played by an orchestra.

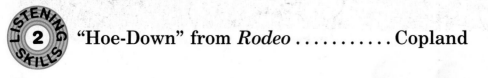

"Hoe-Down" from *Rodeo* . . . . . . . . . . . Copland

## Jumbled and Jivey

Follow the words of this song as you listen to the recording. You may not find out what *Mairzy Doats* means until the middle of the song.

## Mairzy Doats

By Milton Drake, Al Hoffman and Jerry Livingston

Mair - zy doats and do - zy doats and lid - dle lam - zy div - ey,

A kid-dle-y div - ey too, would - n't you? Yes!

Mair - zy doats and do - zy doats and lid - dle lam - zy div - ey,

A kid-dle-y div - ey too, would - n't you?

If the words sound queer, and fun - ny to your ear,

A lit - tle bit jum - bled and jiv - ey, Sing

© 1943 MILLER MUSIC, INC. Copyright renewed and assigned to HALLMARK MUSIC CO., INC. All Rights Reserved. Used by Permission.

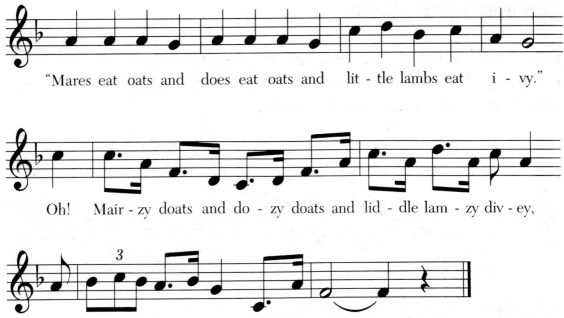

"Mares eat oats and does eat oats and lit - tle lambs eat i - vy."

Oh! Mair - zy doats and do - zy doats and lid - dle lam - zy div - ey,

A kid - dle - y div - ey too, would - n't you? ____

### Eletelephony

Once there was an elephant,
Who tried to use the telephant—
No! no! I mean an elephone
Who tried to use the telephone—
(Dear me! I am not certain quite
That even now I've got it right.)

Howe'er it was, he got his trunk
Entangled in the telephunk;
The more he tried to get it free,
The louder buzzed the telephee—
(I fear I'd better drop the song
Of elephop and telephong!)

*Laura E. Richards*

# Noah's Ark

There are many folk songs about Noah and the ark. In this humorous song, one singer can sing the solo parts. The class can join in on the chorus parts.

## One More River

American Folk Song

1. Old No-ah built him-self an ark, There's one more riv-er to cross,

2. The an-i-mals came two by two,

He built it out of hick-'ry bark, One more riv-er to cross. _

The el-e-phant and kan-ga-roo,

One more riv-er, And that one riv-er is Jor-dan,

One more riv-er, There's one more riv-er to cross. _

3. The animals came three by three,
   There's one more river to cross,
   The baboon and the chimpanzee,
   There's one more river to cross

4. The animals came four by four, . . .
   Old Noah got mad and hollered for more, . . .

5. The animals came five by five, . . .
   The bees came swarming from the hive, .

6. The animals came six by six, . . .
   The lion laughed at the monkey's tricks, . .

7. When Noah found he had no sail, .
   He just ran up his old coat tail, . . .

# A Tongue Twister

The chicken in this song found something new to say.
Listen to the recording to find out what she said.

When the chicken starts to sing her new song, clap
the steady beat in time to the music.

## Chickery Chick

Words and Music by Sylvia Dee and Sidney Lippman

Once there lived a chick-en who would say, "Chick-chick." "Chick-chick" all day.

Soon that chick got sick and tired of just "Chick-chick," _

So one morn-ing she start-ed to say:

"Chick-er-y chick cha-la cha-la, Check-a-la rome-y

in a ba-nan-i-ka, bol-i-ka wol-i-ka can't you see,

Copyright © 1945 Santly Joy, Inc. Copyright renewed and assigned to Harry Von Tilzer Music Publishing Company c/o The Welk Music Group. Santa Monica CA 90401 for the U.S.A.; Chappell & Co., Inc. (Intersong Music, Publisher) for the rest of the world. International Copyright Secured. ALL RIGHTS RESERVED. Used by permission.

**3**           *Fine*

Chick-er-y Chick is me."

Ev - 'ry time you're sick and tired of just the same old thing,

Say - in' just the same old words all day,

Be just like the chick-en who found some-thing new to sing.

*D.S. al Fine*

Op - en up your mouth and start to say, Oh!

# A Musical Conversation

This musical conversation is sung by a solo singer and a chorus. Listen to the recording to find out who sings the solo parts and who sings the chorus parts.

## Who Did?

Black Spiritual

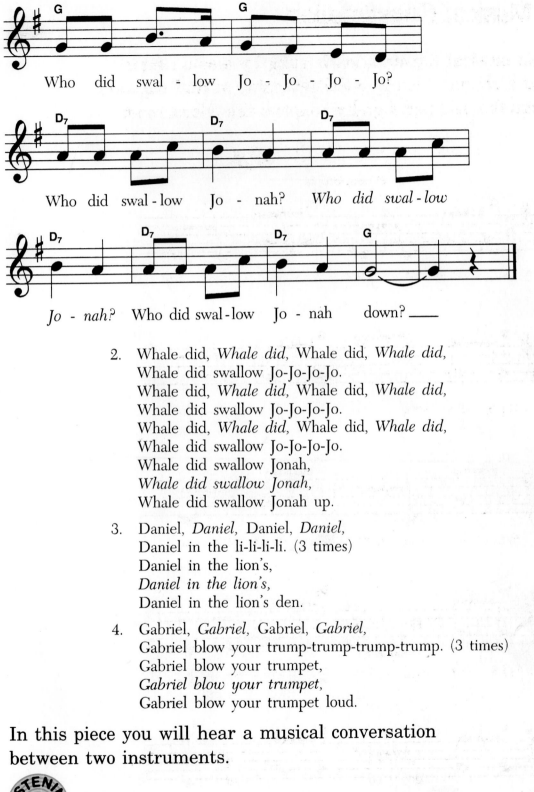

Who did swal-low Jo - Jo - Jo - Jo?

Who did swal-low Jo - nah? *Who did swal-low*

*Jo - nah?* Who did swal-low Jo - nah down? ____

2. Whale did, *Whale did*, Whale did, *Whale did*,
   Whale did swallow Jo-Jo-Jo-Jo.
   Whale did, *Whale did*, Whale did, *Whale did*,
   Whale did swallow Jo-Jo-Jo-Jo.
   Whale did, *Whale did*, Whale did, *Whale did*,
   Whale did swallow Jo-Jo-Jo-Jo.
   Whale did swallow Jonah,
   *Whale did swallow Jonah,*
   Whale did swallow Jonah up.

3. Daniel, *Daniel*, Daniel, *Daniel*,
   Daniel in the li-li-li-li. (3 times)
   Daniel in the lion's,
   *Daniel in the lion's,*
   Daniel in the lion's den.

4. Gabriel, *Gabriel*, Gabriel, *Gabriel*,
   Gabriel blow your trump-trump-trump-trump. (3 times)
   Gabriel blow your trumpet,
   *Gabriel blow your trumpet,*
   Gabriel blow your trumpet loud.

In this piece you will hear a musical conversation
between two instruments.

*Gavotte* . . . . . . . . . . . . . . . . . . . . . . . . . . **Bolling**

# A Story in Music

*The Equatorial Jungle*; Henri ROUSSEAU; National Gallery of Art, Washington; Chester Dale Collection.

**THE EQUATORIAL JUNGLE**
HENRI ROUSSEAU

Maurice Ravel composed a group of pieces called *Mother Goose Suite,* which tells the story of some favorite fairy tales. We know that music cannot tell a story as words do or paint a picture in lines and colors that our real eyes can see. Music can only suggest—make us think of a story or picture.

What does this music suggest to you?

**"The Conversations of Beauty and the Beast"** from *Mother Goose Suite* . . . . . . . . . . . . . Ravel

## The Conversation

At the beginning of the piece, you hear Beauty's voice.

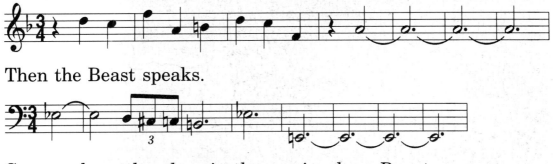

Then the Beast speaks.

Can you hear the place in the music where Beauty
and the Beast talk at the same time?

**Maurice Ravel**
(1875–1937)

Maurice Ravel was born in south-
western France in 1875. Maurice
learned to play the piano when he
was still a child. As he grew older
he became fascinated with the instruments of the orchestra. He
wanted to know how each instrument worked—how it sounded,
how high and how low it could
play. Ravel was also interested in
composing, and before he was 20
years old, he began writing music
of his own.

*Mother Goose Suite* was first written for piano. Later on, when Ravel
rewrote the piece for orchestra, he
was careful to choose the instrument that would best suit each
character in his musical story.

# A Solo-Chorus Song

Listen to the solo parts and join in on the chorus parts.

## All Night, All Day

Black Spiritual

Can you find this pattern in the song?
Can you play it on the bells?
The pattern starts on the D bell.

# Add a Verse

Look at the music in the color box. Can you find another phrase that looks exactly like it?

## He's Got the Whole World in His Hands

Black Spiritual

1. He's got the whole world in his hands,

He's got the whole world in his hands,

He's got the whole world in his hands,

He's got the whole world in his hands.

2. He's got the wind and rain in his hands, (3 times)
He's got the whole world in his hands.

3. He's got both you and me in his hands, (3 times)
He's got the whole world in his hands.

4. He's got everybody in his hands, (3 times)
He's got the whole world in his hands.

Make up a new verse to sing with the melody of "He's Got the Whole World in His Hands." Teach your classmates to sing your new verse.

# Careers in Music

Kim and Reggie Harris make music
in many places. These pictures show
them in a studio, on a stage,
and in a classroom.

*Careers in Music*
........ Kim and
Reggie Harris

53

# Bicycle Built for Two

This song has been a favorite for almost 100 years.
Heads still turn when a bicycle built for two goes by.

## Daisy Bell

Words and Music by Harry Dacre

Dai - sy, Dai - sy, Give me your an - swer, do; _____

I'm half cra - zy, All for the love of you. _____

It won't be a styl - ish mar - riage; ___

I can't af - ford a car - riage, ___

But you'll look sweet up - on the seat of a

bi - cy - cle built for two. _____

## Percussion Accompaniment

The woodblock and triangle can play an "oom-pah-pah" accompaniment for "Daisy Bell." Which part will you try? Team up with a friend and practice on your own.

## A Song About Smiles

When you smile, it usually means you are happy. When you smile, you make other people happy, too. Put a smile in your voice when you sing this happy song.

## Smile That Smile

Words and Music by Carmino Ravosa

Smile that smile, You can, I know you.

Smile that smile, Don't let things throw you.

Smile that smile, Just look, I'll show you that way. _____

Laugh that laugh, Just let me hear it.

Laugh that laugh, Just let me near it.

© 1985 Carmino Ravosa

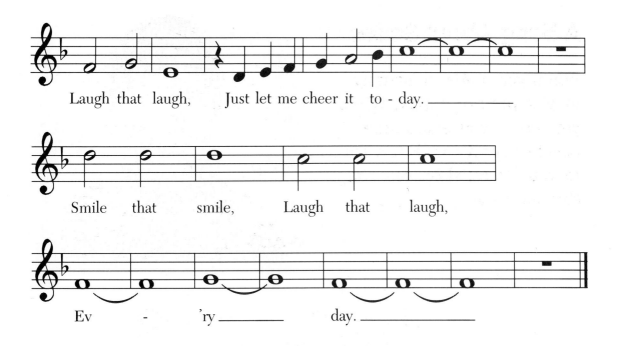

Laugh that laugh,    Just let me cheer it to - day. _____

Smile    that    smile,    Laugh    that    laugh,

Ev - 'ry _____    day. _____

## Find the Melody Pattern

How many times do you see this melody pattern in
"Smile that Smile"? Use the bells and play the
pattern every time it comes in the song.

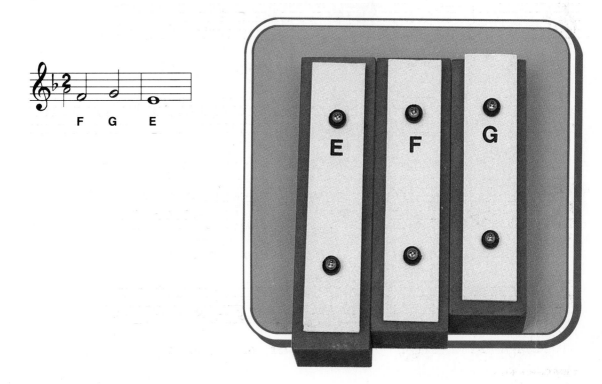

F  G  E

# A Song that Never Ends

This is a song from a movie called *Bambi*. Bambi was a fawn who lived in the forest with a rabbit named Thumper and a skunk named Flower.

At the beginning of the movie, all the creatures of the forest are living happily together, and this is the song they sing.

## Love Is a Song

Words by Larry Morey     Music by Frank Churchill

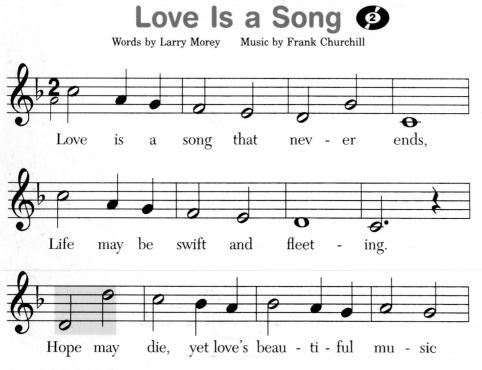

Love    is    a    song    that    nev - er    ends,

Life    may    be    swift    and    fleet - ing.

Hope    may    die,    yet    love's    beau - ti - ful    mu - sic

© 1942 Wonderland Music, Co., Inc.

comes each day like the dawn. _____

Love is a song that nev - er ends;

One sim - ple theme re - peat - ing.

Like the voice of a heav - en - ly choir, _

love's sweet mu - sic flows on. _____

# The Message of the Bells

There were many churches in old London Town. Most of the churches had big bells in their towers. Sometimes the bells rang out the time of day. At other times the bells announced an important event.

What messages do the bells give in this old English folk song?

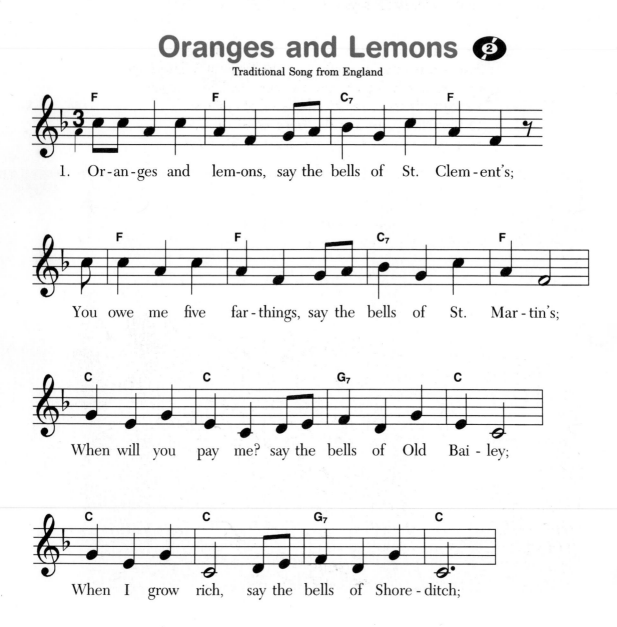

## Oranges and Lemons

Traditional Song from England

1. Or-an-ges and lem-ons, say the bells of St. Clem-ent's;

You owe me five far-things, say the bells of St. Mar-tin's;

When will you pay me? say the bells of Old Bai-ley;

When I grow rich, say the bells of Shore-ditch;

When will that be? — say the bells of Step - ney; —

I do not know — says the great bell of Bow.

2. Pancakes and fritters, say the bells of St. Peter's;
   Two sticks and an apple, say the bells of Whitechapel;
   Old Father Baldpate, say the slow bells of Aldgate;
   Poker and tongs, say the bells of St. John's;
   Kettles and pans, say the bells of St. Ann's;
   Brickbats and tiles, say the bells of St. Giles.

**BOSTON**
**ALBERT GOODWIN**

## Bell Introductions

Listen for the bell tune that is played
as an introduction to the song.

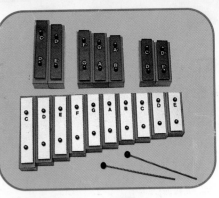

# The Little Bells of Westminster 3️⃣

### Traditional Round

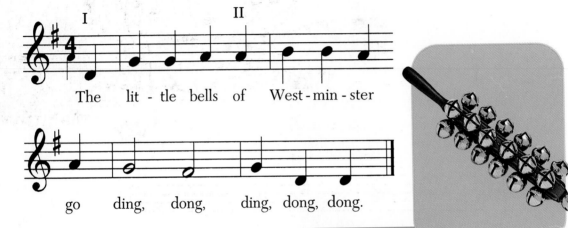

I          II

The    lit - tle bells of    West - min - ster

go     ding,    dong,    ding, dong, dong.

Which bell tune will you play
as an introduction to "The
Little Bells of Westminster"?

G

G   D

G   D

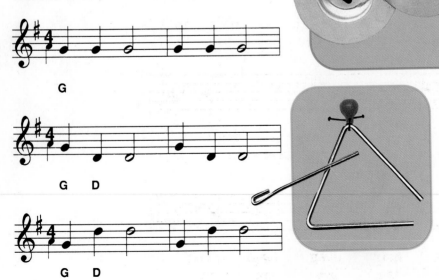

## Evening Bells

Play a ringing sound on a triangle or on the finger cymbals to accompany this song.

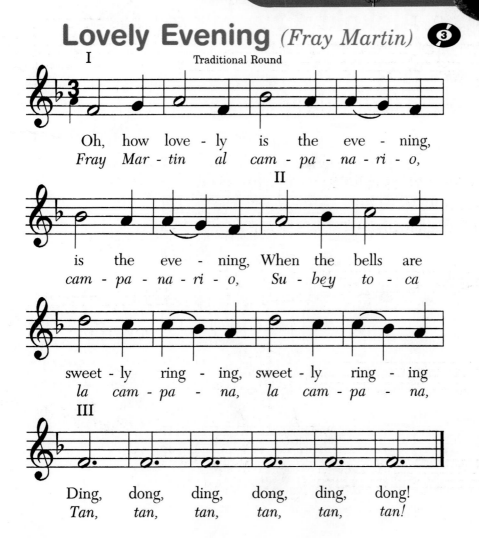

## Lovely Evening (Fray Martin)

**I**

Traditional Round

Oh, how love - ly is the eve - ning,
*Fray Mar - tin al cam - pa - na - ri - o,*

**II**

is the eve - ning, When the bells are
*cam - pa - na - ri - o, Su - bey to - ca*

sweet - ly ring - ing, sweet - ly ring - ing
*la cam - pa - na, la cam - pa - na,*

**III**

Ding, dong, ding, dong, ding, dong!
*Tan, tan, tan, tan, tan, tan!*

# A Chant from Hawaii

Pat your knees or clap your hands in time to the music of this Hawaiian chant.

## Alekoki ③

Hawaiian Chant    English Version by Aura Kontra

Oh,    is there such  a  place of  beau - ty
*A - o - le    i   pi - li - wi    i  -  a,*

As  the  crys - tal pools of  A - le - ko - ki,
*Ka - hi  wa - i   a - o   A - le - ko - ki,*

Where for - est shad - ows  fall  so  gent - ly
*Ho - o - ko - hu  ka 'u - a   i    u  -  ka,*

In  the  si - lence of  the  hid - den  val - ley?
*No - ho  ma - i   la  i  Nu - u - a  -  nu.*

# Song of the Burrito

The *burrito* in this song can walk, talk, and even eat with a fork!

## Tinga Layo

Calypso from the West Indies    English Version by Margaret Marks

**REFRAIN**

Tin - ga  Lay  -  o!
Run, lit - tle don - key,  run!
*¡Ven,  mi  bu - rri - to,  ven!*

Tin - ga  Lay  -  o!
Run, lit - tle don - key,  run!  run!
*¡Ven,  mi  bu - rri - to,  ven!  ven!*

1.–3. | Last time only

**VERSE**

1. My don - key    yes,    my don - key    no,
1. *Bu - rri - to    sí,    bu - rri - to    no.*

My don - key    stop when    I  tell him to    go!
*¡Bu - rri - to    co - me  con  te - ne  -  dor!*

2.  My donkey hee, my donkey haw,
    My donkey sit on the kitchen floor! *Refrain*

3.  My donkey kick, my donkey balk,
    My donkey eat with a silver fork! *Refrain*

## Lullaby from Puerto Rico

A lullaby is a love song sung by a mother
to her child. Can you think of a word that
will tell how a lullaby should be sung?

# Go to Sleep, My Treasure

Folk Song from Puerto Rico

1. Oh, go to sleep, my trea - sure, Oh, go to sleep, my trea - sure,
2. Oh, hush - a - by, my ba - by, Oh, hush - a - by, my ba - by,
*Du - er - ma - se, ri - cu - ra, Du - er - ma - se, mi ni - no,*

For all the lit - tle an - gels are watch - ing from the skies. —
For all the lit - tle an - gels are watch - ing ov - er you. —
*Que los — an - ge - li - tos Mi - ran - do - te es - tan. —*

Oh, go to sleep, my trea - sure, Oh, go to sleep, my trea - sure,
Oh, hush - a - by, my ba - by, Oh, hush - a - by, my ba - by,
*Du - er - ma - se, ri - cu - ra, Du - er - ma - se, mi ni - no,*

The night is grow - ing dark, and it's time to close your eyes. ____
The lit - tle guar - dian an - gels will watch the whole night through. _
*Que la no - che ob - scu - ra, Du - er - ma - se, ri cu - ra.*

From LULLABIES OF THE WORLD, by Dorothy Berliner Commins. Copyright © 1967 by Dorothy Berliner Commins. Reprinted by permission of Random House, Inc.

Listen for the lullaby melody in this piece.

**3** LISTENING SKILLS *Trumpeter's Lullaby* . . . . . . . . . . . . . **Anderson**

# Fiesta Time

On the seventh of July, people of Spanish origin sing this song to celebrate the fiesta in honor of the Spanish Saint Fermin.

## The First of January *Uno de enero*

Folk Song from Mexico

First of the first month, sec-ond of the sec-ond month, Third of the
*U - no de e - ne - ro, dos __ de fe - bre - ro, tres __ de*

third, and fourth of the fourth; Fifth of the fifth month, sixth of the
*mar - zo, cua - tro de a - bril, cin - co de ma - yo, seis __ de*

sixth month, Sev-enth of Ju - ly is San Fer - min.
*ju - nio, sie - te de ju - lio, San Fer - mín.*

La, la, la, la, la, la, la, Tam-bour-ine's brok-en, we can-not play it.
*¿quién __ ha ro - to la pan-de - re - ta?*

La, la, la, la, la, la, la, If you broke it, you must re-place it.
*el que la ha ro - to la pa-ga - rá. __*

This song tells you how to count from one to seven in Spanish: *uno, dos, tres, cuatro, cinco, seis, siete.*

Reprinted from CANTEMOS EN ESPAÑOL (KL10) Copyright 1961 Max & Beatrice Krone, Neil A. Kjos Music Company, Publisher. Reprinted with permission 1986.

You will hear seven songs. When a number is called, listen to the music. Then on your worksheet, write a check mark in the blank after the correct answer.

**1.** It is a cowhand's song. ____
It is a sailor's song. ____

**2.** It is a song about farming. ____
It is an American Indian chant. ____

**3.** It is a railroad song. ____
It is an American Indian chant. ____

**4.** It is a song of the sea. ____
It is a song a cowhand sings. ____

**5.** It is a song about farming. ____
It is a song about a railroad. ____

**6.** It is a railroad song. ____
It is a song a cowhand sings. ____

**7.** It is a sailor's work song. ____
It is an American Indian chant. ____

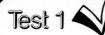

After each number you will find words that describe a song in your book. From the song list, choose the song that fits each description and, on your worksheet, write its letter in the blank.

**1.** A song that was composed by Woody Guthrie _____

**2.** A song that comes from an American Indian tribe _____

**3.** A song that American cowhands sang _____

**4.** A song that is a sea shantey _____

**5.** A song that is used as an American square-dance tune _____

**6.** A song that has solo parts and chorus parts _____

**7.** A song that was sung by Norwegian farmers _____

**8.** A song that was sung by Newfoundland fishermen _____

**A.** I'se the B'y

**B.** Pop, Goes the Weasel

**C.** This Land Is Your Land

**D.** Oleana

**E.** My Home's in Montana

**F.** H'Atira

**G.** Johnny, Come to Hilo

**H.** One More River

After each song title you will find two words.
Circle the word that best describes how the song
should be sung.

1. This Land Is Your Land      joyfully      quietly

2. All Night, All Day      quietly      quickly

3. Blow, Ye Winds      calmly      energetically

4. Grandma's Farm      merrily      sadly

5. Old Joe Clark      sadly      cheerfully

6. Who Did?      slowly      lively

7. Chickery Chick      humorously      sadly

8. Buffalo Gals      lively      calmly

9. Daisy Bell      heavily      lightly

10. Love Is a Song      smoothly      jaggedly

You will hear selections from the Listening Library. When a number is called, read the sentence next to the number and listen to the music. If you think the statement is true, circle the word TRUE on your worksheet. If the statement is false, circle the word FALSE.

**1.** This is the beginning of Copland's "Circus Music."
            TRUE      FALSE

**2.** This is the B section of "Circus Music"; it ends with loud chords.
            TRUE      FALSE

**3.** This is Beauty's theme from "The Conversations of Beauty and the Beast."
            TRUE      FALSE

**4.** This is Beauty's theme from "The Conversations of Beauty and the Beast."
            TRUE      FALSE

**5.** In this music, the melody is played by a clarinet.
            TRUE      FALSE

**6.** This music starts slow and gets faster.
            TRUE      FALSE

**7.** In this music you hear a piano and a trumpet.
            TRUE      FALSE

**8.** In this music the melody is played by a trumpet.
            TRUE      FALSE

# UNDERSTANDING MUSIC

## Tempo: Fast—Slow

Which picture shows a rider moving fast?

What does the other picture show?

Listen to this song. Which part is fast?
Which part is slow?

# Stodola Pumpa ③

Czechoslovakian Folk Song     Words Adapted

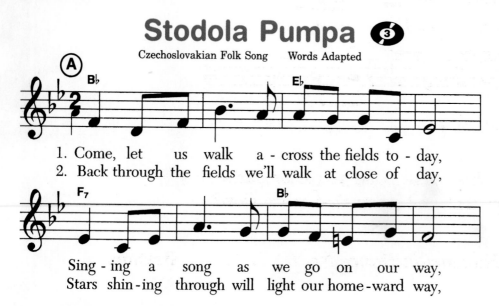

1. Come, let us walk a - cross the fields to - day,
2. Back through the fields we'll walk at close of day,

Sing - ing a song as we go on our way,
Stars shin - ing through will light our home - ward way,

Come, let us walk a - cross the fields to - day,
Back through the fields we'll walk at close of day

Sing - ing a song as we go on our way. — Hey!
Stars shin - ing through will light our home - ward way. —

**B** REFRAIN

Sto - do - la, sto - do - la, sto - do - la pum - pa,

Sto - do - la pum - pa, sto - do - la pum - pa,

Sto - do - la, sto - do - la, sto - do - la pum - pa,

Sto - do - la pum - pa, pum, pum, pum.

Listen to this music. Can you hear parts
that move fast and parts that move slow?

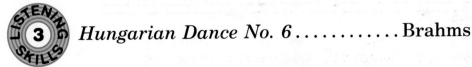

**3** *Hungarian Dance No. 6* . . . . . . . . . . . Brahms

## Tempo: Faster—Slower

Each of the objects pictured above can get faster and slower. Can you name other objects that can get faster and slower?

What happens to the tempo in this song? Does the music get faster? Slower?

## Dancing 3

Czechoslovakian Folk Song

Come and dance, turn light - ly, turn light - ly,

A - round the camp - fire burn - ing so bright - ly,

The snow falls fast, and cold is the weath-er,

Come dance, come dance, we'll all turn to-geth-er.

La la la la, La la la la,

La la la la, La la la la la,

La la la la, La la la la,

La la la la, La la la la la la la la la.

What happens to the tempo in this piece for orchestra?

LISTENING SKILLS **3** "Pizzicato Polka" from *Ballet Suite No. 1* . . . . . . . . . . . . . . . . . . . . . . . Shostakovich

Pat your knees or clap your hands
in time to the music of this song.

## I'd 've Baked a Cake

Words and Music by Al Hoffman, Bob Merrill and Clem Watts

If I knew you were com-in' I'd-'ve baked a cake, -
Had you dropped me a let-ter I'd-'ve hired a band, -

baked a cake, _ baked a cake, _ If I
grand-est band _ in the land, _ Had you

knew you were com-in' I'd-'ve baked a cake, _
dropped me a let-ter I'd-'ve hired a band, _

**1.**

How-ja do, how-ja do, how-ja do.

**2.**

And spread the wel-come mat for you. ___

© 1950 by EMI-Music Publishing, Ltd. © Copyright Renewed 1978 by EMI-Music Publishing Ltd. All Rights for the U.S. and Canada controlled by Colgems-EMI Music, Inc. Hollywood, CA 90028.

Now I don't know where you came ___ from _ 'cause I
don't know where you've been, ___ But it
real - ly does - n't mat - ter, grab a chair and fill your plat - ter
And dig dig dig right in, ___ If I
knew you were com - in' I'd -'ve baked a cake, _
hired a band, _ good - ness sake! _ If I
knew you were com - in' I'd -'ve baked a cake, __
How - ja do, how - ja do, how - ja do.

## Sets of Two

Let your hands march left-right, left-right, as you listen to "The German Band." You might want to chant softly the words *left-right, left-right,* as the music goes along.

# The German Band

German Folk Song    English Words by Margaret Marks

REFRAIN

Come and hear the Ger-man band, Ger-man band, Ger-man band!

Oh, the weath-er is so grand for the big pa-rade!

1. First there comes a drum-mer, And as a drum-mer,

He's quite a plumb-er! He's off the beat in ev-'ry

num-ber, And no one knows how come They let him drum. ___

80

2. Next come brasses playing,
   It sounds like neighing,
   Or donkeys braying!
   And all the people there are saying,
   "Let's stuff 'em up with hay
   So they won't play!" *Refrain*

3. Next comes our police force,
   Three men and one horse,
   I wonder who's boss!
   Although their leader shouts his head off,
   With his *a-hep, a-hep,*
   They're out of step! *Refrain*

## Pick a Pattern

You can chant or play an instrument to accompany
"The German Band." Will you chant or play?

Chant

Left right, left right, left right, left right,

Drum

Cymbals

Listen for beats in sets of two in this music.

LISTENING SKILLS 4

"March" from *The Nutcracker Suite* . . . . . . . .
. . . . . . . . . . . . . . . . . . . . . . . . . . . Tchaikovsky

# Sets of Two—Meter in 2

Which row of symbols shows the steady beat? Which row shows the beats in sets of two?

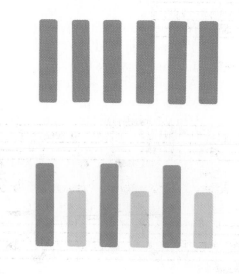

To feel the beats moving in sets of two, pretend to strum a banjo as you listen to this song. Strum down-up, down-up, across the strings.

## Boil Them Cabbage Down

American Pioneer Song

1. The rac-coon's got a fur - ry tail,

The pos-sum's tail is bare, _

From MORE SONGS OF THE NEW WORLD by Desmond MacMahon. Published by Holmes McDougall Ltd.

The rab-bit ain't got no tail at all,

But a lit-tle bit o' bunch o' hair.

**B** REFRAIN

Boil them cab-bage down, down, Bake them bis-cuits brown, brown,

The on-ly tune I ev-er did learn is Boil them cab-bage down.

2. The June bug he has wings of gold,
   The firefly wings of flame,
   The bedbug's got no wings at all,
   But he gets there just the same. *Refrain*

3. Oh, love it is a killing fit
   When beauty hits a blossom,
   And if you want your finger bit,
   Just poke it at a possum. *Refrain*

## Steady Beat—Strong Beat

Play the steady beat
on a woodblock.

Play the strong beat
on a drum.

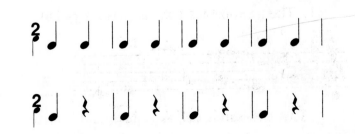

## Sets of Three

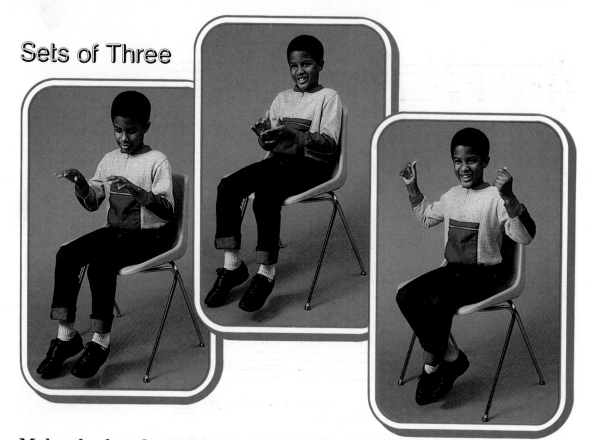

Make the hand motions shown in the pictures as you listen to this old, favorite song.

# Take Me Out to the Ball Game 🄸

Words by Jack Norworth    Music by Albert von Tilzer

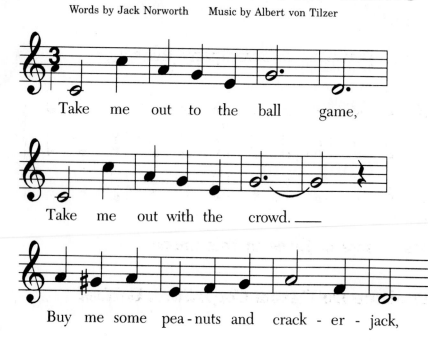

Take me out to the ball game,

Take me out with the crowd. ____

Buy me some pea - nuts and crack - er - jack,

I don't care if we nev-er get back,

Let me root, root, root for the home team,

If they don't win it's a shame, ___

For it's one, two, three strikes you're out

At the old ball game. ___

## Pick a Pattern

Which pattern will you play to accompany the song?

Woodblock

Tambourine

Drum

Listen for beats in sets of three in this music.

"Waltz of the Doll" from *Coppelia* . . . Delibes

# Sets of Three—Meter in 3

The top row of symbols shows the steady beat. What does the bottom row show?

What sign tells you that this pattern moves in a meter of 3? Tap the pattern as you listen to "Springfield Mountain."

## Springfield Mountain

American Folk Song

G          D₇

1. On Spring-field Moun-tain there did dwell
2. This love-li youth one day did go

D₇                    G

A love-li youth; I knowed him well. ____
Down to the mead-ow for to mow. ____

Too loo - re - ay, too loo - re - oo,

Too loo - re - ay, too loo - re - oo.

3. He scarce had mowed quite round the field
   When a cruel sarpent bit his heel.

4. They took him home to Molli dear
   Which made him feel so very queer.

5. Now Molli had two ruby lips
   With which the p'ison she did sip.

6. Now Molli had a rotting tooth
   And so the p'ison killed them both.

## Steady Beat—Strong Beat

Play the steady beat on a woodblock.

Play the strong beat on a drum.

# Short Sounds—Long Sounds

Follow the music as you listen to this song. Notice the notes in the color boxes. Do you hear the *Billy Boy* pattern anywhere else in the song?

## Billy Boy

English Folk Song

1. Oh, __ where have you been, Bil-ly Boy, Bil-ly Boy?
2. Did she bid you to come in, Bil-ly Boy, Bil-ly Boy?

Oh, __ where have you been, charm-ing Bil-ly? I have
Did she bid you to come in, charm-ing Bil-ly? Yes, she

been to seek a wife, She's the joy __ of my life,
bid me to come in, There's a dim-ple in her chin,

She's a young thing and can-not leave her moth-er. _____

3. Did she give you a chair, Billy Boy, Billy Boy?
   Yes, she gave me a chair, but there was no bottom there,

4. Can she make a cherry pie, Billy Boy, Billy Boy?
   She can make a cherry pie, quick as a cat can wink her eye,

5. Can she cook and can she spin, Billy Boy, Billy Boy?
   She can cook and she can spin, she can do most anything,

6. How old is she, Billy Boy, Billy Boy?
   Three times six and four times seven, twenty-eight and eleven,

88

# Chant, Clap, Play

CHANT the *Billy Boy* pattern several times.

Bil-ly Boy, Bil-ly Boy, Bil-ly Boy, Bil-ly Boy

CLAP the *Billy Boy* pattern several times. Say *short-short-long* as you clap.

▬ ▬ ▬▬ ▬ ▬ ▬ ▬▬ ▬ ▬ ▬ ▬▬ ▬ ▬

PLAY the *Billy Boy* pattern on a woodblock.

## Chant a Pattern

1. <u>John</u> <u>John</u> <u>Mar-y</u> <u>Mar-y</u>

2. <u>Car-los</u> <u>Car-los</u> <u>Jane</u> <u>Jane</u>

3. <u>Bet-ty</u> <u>Joe</u> <u>Bet-ty</u> <u>Joe</u>

4. <u>Jer-ry</u> <u>Jer-ry</u> <u>Jer-ry</u> <u>Beth</u>

## Play a Pattern

Make up your own pattern of short and long sounds.

# Long—Short

Follow the music as you listen to the recording. Do the notes in the color boxes show long sounds or short sounds?

## Louisiana Lullaby

Folk Song from Louisiana

1. Dream-land o-pens here, Sweep the dream path clear.

Lis-ten child, now lis-ten well,

What the tor-toise may have to tell,

What the tor-toise may have to tell.

2. Dreamland opens here,
   Sweep the dream path clear.
   Listen child, dear little child,
   To the song of the crocodile,
   To the song of the crocodile.

3. Dreamland opens here,
   Sweep the dream path clear.
   Listen child, now close your eyes,
   In the cane-break the wild cat cries,
   In the cane-break the wild cat cries.

From SING IT YOURSELF by Dorothy Gordon, copyright 1928, 1933 by E. P. Dutton, renewed 1956, 1961 by Dorothy Gordon. Reprinted by permission of the publisher, E. P. Dutton, a division of New American Library.

# Sound and Silence

In music, sounds are shown with notes.
Find these notes in "Louisiana Lullaby."

In music, silences are shown with rests.
Find these rests in "Louisiana Lullaby."

Look at the chart, and answer the questions below.

• How many eighth notes can take the place of a quarter note?

• How many quarter notes can take the place of a half note?

• How many quarter notes can take the place of a dotted half note?

• How many quarter notes can take the place of a whole note?

Listen for longer and shorter sounds in this music.

*The Skater's Waltzes* . . . . . . . . . . . . Waldteufel

# How Tones Move: Repeated Tones

Look at the notes in the color box. Do they move upward or downward, or do they stay the same?

Follow the music as you listen to the song. Can you find three other places where the tones repeat like those in the color box?

## Deep in the Heart of Texas

Words by June Hershey    Music by Don Swander

The stars at night are big and bright,

Deep in the heart of Tex-as; _____

The prai - rie sky is wide and high,

Deep in the heart of Tex-as. _____

The sage in bloom is like per - fume,

© 1941 Melody Lane Publications, Inc. Used by permission.

Deep in the heart of Tex - as; _____

Re - minds me of the one I love,

Deep in the heart of Tex - as. _____

**Play the repeated tones every time they come in the song.**

Bells

# How Tones Move: Upward by Step

Look at the notes in the color box. Do they move upward or downward, or do they stay the same?

Follow the music as you listen to the song. Can you find another place where the tones move upward by step like those in the color box?

## Sheep Shearing

Swedish Folk Song     English Words by Sam Blum

VERSE

1. Go  get  the sheep, we're clip-ping to-day,
2. Tell Moth-er  dear  we're card-ing  to-day,

Clip-ping their wool, yes,  clip-ping their wool
Card-ing  the  wool, yes, card-ing  the  wool

So    we can knit some stock-ings for  you,
So    we can knit  a    scarf  for  her, too,

Then   we shall dance till  morn-ing.
Then   we shall dance till  morn-ing.

**REFRAIN**

Surr, surr, surr, surr, surr, surr, Wheel spins a-round, round and a-round,

Surr, surr, surr, surr, surr, surr, Then we shall dance till morn-ing.

3. Tell brother John we're spinning today,
   Spinning the wool, yes, spinning the wool
   So we can knit a lace for his shoe,
   Then we shall dance till morning.

4. Tell sister Jane we're dyeing today,
   Dyeing the wool, yes, dyeing the wool
   So we can knit a sweater of blue,
   Then we shall dance till morning.

**Play the tones that move upward by step every time they come in the song.**

Bells

# How Tones Move: Downward by Step

Look at the notes in the color box. Do they move upward or downward, or do they stay the same?

Follow the music as you listen to the song. Can you find three other places where the tones move downward like those in the color box?

## Nine Red Horsemen

Folk Melody from Mexico    Words by Eleanor Farjeon

1. I ___ saw nine red horse-men ride _ o - ver the plain,
2. Their _ hair streamed be - hind them, their _ eyes were a - shine;
3. Their _ spurs clinked and jin - gled, their _ laugh -ter was gay,

And _ each gripped his horse ___ by its long flow -ing mane.
They _ all rode as one man al - though they were nine.
And _ in the red sun - set they _ gal - loped a - way.

Ho hil -lo, hil -lo, hil -lo ho! Ho hil -lo, hil -lo, hil -lo ho!

Ho hil -lo, hil -lo, hil -lo ho! Ho hil -lo, hil -lo, hil -lo ho!

From ELEANOR FARJEON'S POEMS FOR CHILDREN. Originally published in SING FOR YOUR SUPPER by Eleanor Farjeon, copyright 1938 by Eleanor Farjeon, renewed 1966 by Gervase Farjeon. By permission of J. B. Lippincott, Publishers and Harold Ober Associates, Incorporated.

Play each pattern of tones that
move downward by step.

Bells

E

D

C

B

# How Tones Move: Up and Down by Leap

Look at the notes in the color box. Do they move by step, do they stay the same, or do they leap?

## The Unbirthday Song

Words and Music by Mack David, Al Hoffman and Jerry Livingston

1. A ver-y mer-ry un-birth-day to you, to you.
2. A ver-y mer-ry un-birth-day to us, to us.

A ver-y mer-ry un-birth-day to you, to you.
A ver-y mer-ry un-birth-day to us, to us.

It's great to share with some-one and I guess that you will do;
If there are no ob-jec-tions, let it be u-nan-i-mous;

A ver-y mer-ry un-birth-day to you. _____
A ver-y mer-ry un-birth-day to us. _____

3. A very merry unbirthday to all, to all.
   A very merry unbirthday to all, to all.
   Let's have a celebration, hire a band and rent a hall;
   A very merry unbirthday to all.

Bells

Play the large leap downward when it comes in the song.

C    C

© 1948 Walt Disney Music Company. Reprinted with permission.

**98**

## Steps, Leaps, Repeats

Here are parts of songs you may know. Look at the music to see when the notes repeat, and when they move upward or downward by step or by leap. Try playing the parts on bells.

## Two Pieces for Piano

The two pieces you will
hear were composed by
Robert Schumann. They
are among the best-known
and best-loved piano pieces
of all times. Children
play the pieces for family
and friends. Famous
pianists play the pieces in
concert halls all over
the world.

As you listen to the music, look at the words in the
two lists below. Which list of words suggests the
mood, or feeling, of the music in the first piece?
In the second piece?

|          |          |
|----------|----------|
| cheerful | quiet    |
| jolly    | peaceful |
| lively   | restful  |

 "The Happy Farmer" from *The Album for
the Young* . . . . . . . . . . . . . . . . . . . . . . Schumann

 "Dreaming" from *Scenes from Childhood* . . .
. . . . . . . . . . . . . . . . . . . . . . . . . . . . Schumann

Here is the melody you hear at the beginning
of "The Happy Farmer."

You hear this melody at the beginning of "Dreaming."

**Robert Schumann**
**(1810–1856)**

Just one year after Abraham Lincoln was born in Kentucky, a baby boy named Robert Schumann was born in a German village near Leipzig, which was at that time the music capital of the world. Lincoln grew up to be President of the United States; Schumann became one of Germany's finest composers.

Schumann studied piano with Herr Weick, one of the best piano teachers of his day. It was for Herr Weick's daughter Clara that Schumann wrote *Scenes from Childhood,* a series of 12 piano pieces, including "Traümerei" (the German word for *dreaming*).

# Follow the Phrase Lines

Notice the phrase lines above the music. As you
listen to the recording, trace with your finger the rise
and fall of each phrase line.

How many phrases does this melody have?

## Down in the Valley

Kentucky Folk Song

1. Down in the val - ley, val - ley so low,
2. Build me a cas - tle for - ty feet high,

Hang your head o - ver, hear the wind blow,
So I can see you as you pass by.

Hear the wind blow, dear, hear the wind blow,
As you ride by, dear, as you ride by,

Hang your head o - ver, hear the wind blow.
So I can see you as you ride by.

3. Writing a letter, containing three lines,
Answer my question: "Will you be mine?"
Will you be mine, dear, will you be mine.
Answer my question: "Will you be mine?"

# Phrase Length

Follow the phrase lines as you listen to "Peace Like a River." Are the phrases all the same length, or are some long and some short?

## Peace Like a River

Traditional

2. I've got joy like a fountain, *(2 times)*
   I've got joy like a fountain in my soul.
   I've got joy like a fountain, *(2 times)*
   I've got joy like a fountain in my soul.

3. I've got love like the ocean, *(2 times)*
   I've got love like the ocean in my soul.
   I've got love like the ocean, *(2 times)*
   I've got love like the ocean in my soul.

What can you discover about the phrases in this poem?

### A Modern Dragon

A train is a dragon that roars through the dark.
He wriggles his tail as he sends up a spark.
He pierces the night with his one yellow eye,
And all the earth trembles when he rushes by.

*Rowena Bastin Bennett*

# Melody and Harmony

You will hear two performances of a song in your book. As you listen to the recording, decide which picture shows what is happening in each performance.

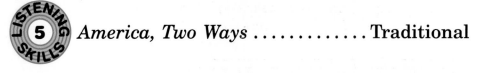 *America, Two Ways* . . . . . . . . . . . . . Traditional

## Two Ways to Make Harmony

Add harmony to "Brother John" by playing chords on an autoharp. As the class sings the melody, play the F chord all through the song.

# Brother John
## (Frère Jacques)

Traditional French Round

Are you sleep - ing, Are you sleep - ing?
*Frè - re    Jac - ques,    Frè - re    Jac - ques,*

Broth - er    John,    Broth - er    John?
*Dor - mez    vous,    Dor - mez    vous?*

Morn-ing bells are ring-ing, Morn-ing bells are sing-ing,
*Son-nez les  ma - ti - nes, Son-nez les  ma - ti - nes,*

Ding   ding   dong,   Ding   ding   dong.
*Din    din    don,    Din    din    don.*

## Ostinatos

Add harmony by singing or playing a repeated
pattern (ostinato) all through the song. As the class
sings the melody, try one of these ostinatos.

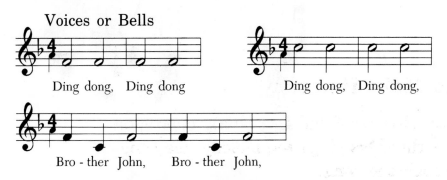

Voices or Bells

Ding dong,  Ding dong

Ding dong,  Ding dong,

Bro - ther John,   Bro - ther John,

# Partner Songs

Listen to the recording of two American folk songs. One is printed on this page; the other, on the next page. Follow the music of each song as you listen.

## Sandy Land

Folk Song from Oklahoma

1. Make my liv-in' in sand - y land,

Make my liv-in' in sand - y land,

Make my liv-in' in sand - y land,

La - dies, fare you well.

2. Raise sweet potatoes in sandy land, *(3 times)*
   Ladies, fare you well.

3. Dig sweet potatoes in sandy land, *(3 times)*
   Ladies, fare you well.

4. Make my livin' in sandy land, *(3 times)*
   Ladies, fare you well.

Add harmony to the melody of "Sandy Land" by playing the autoharp chords.

Reprinted by permission of Curtis Brown, Ltd. Copyright © 1937, 1963 by B. A. Botkin.

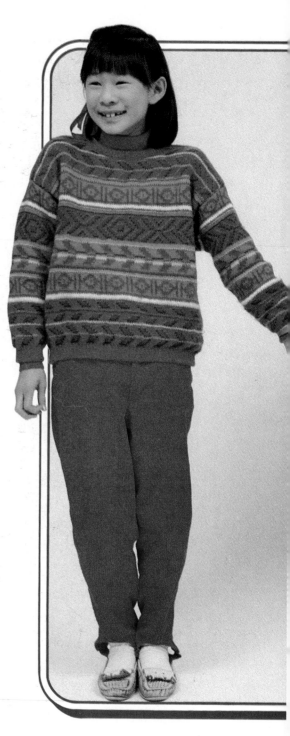

# Bow, Belinda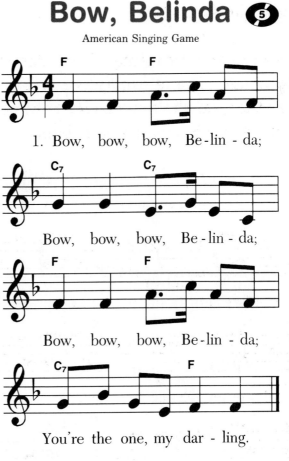

American Singing Game

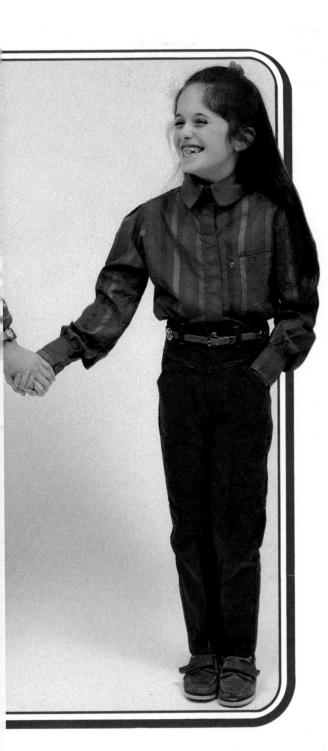

1. Bow, bow, bow, Be-lin-da;

Bow, bow, bow, Be-lin-da;

Bow, bow, bow, Be-lin-da;

You're the one, my dar-ling.

2. Right hand round, Oh, Belinda; *(3 times)*
   You're the one, my darling.

3. Left hand round, Oh, Belinda; *(3 times)*
   You're the one, my darling.

4. Both hands round, Oh, Belinda; *(3 times)*
   You're the one, my darling.

## Putting Two Songs Together

While some of your classmates sing "Sandy Land," others can sing "Bow, Belinda."

Singing partner songs is one way to create harmony.

# Follow the Leader

Listen for the voices playing follow-the-leader in the recording of this song.

## Make New Friends ⑤

Make new friends, but keep the old,

One is sil-ver and the oth-er gold.

When your class can sing the melody of "Make New Friends" without the recording, try singing the song as a two-part round.

## A Two-Part Round

When your class knows the melody of "Scotland's Burning," divide into two groups and sing the song as a two-part round.

### Scotland's Burning

Round

I
Scot-land's burn-ing, Scot-land's burn-ing,

II
Look out, Look out, Fire! Fire! Fire! Fire!

Pour on wa-ter, Pour on wa-ter!

## Add an Ostinato

Add an ostinato to a performance of "Scotland's Burning." Will you sing the ostinato, or play it on the bells?

Wa - ter, Wa - ter

# Two Melodies Together

Harmony is created when two melodies are sung at the same time. Listen for the harmony part on this recording of "Sandy Land."

## Sandy Land

Folk Song from Oklahoma

1. Make my liv-in' in sand-y land,
   Make my liv-in' in sand-y land,
   Make my liv-in' in sand-y land,
   La-dies, fare you well.

2. Raise sweet potatoes in sandy land, *(3 times)*
   Ladies, fare you well.

3. Dig sweet potatoes in sandy land, *(3 times)*
   Ladies, fare you well.

4. Make my livin' in sandy land, *(3 times)*
   Ladies, fare you well.

Reprinted by permission of Curtis Brown, Ltd. Copyright © 1937, 1963 by B. A. Botkin.

### Countermelody

Sand-y land, Sand-y land, Sand-y land, Fare you well.

## Add a Countermelody

Listen for the countermelody in the recording of "Roll on the Ground."

# Roll on the Ground

Folk Song from Mississippi

REFRAIN

Roll on    the ground, boys,   roll on    the ground,

Roll on    the ground, boys,   roll on    the ground.

VERSE

1. Work on    the rail - road,   sleep on    the ground,
2. Work on    the rail - road,   work all    the day,

*D.C. al Fine*

Eat so - dy crack - ers, and the wind blow them a-round.
Eat so - dy crack - ers, and the wind blow them a - way.

Transcribed and Adapted from the Library of Congress Field Recordings AFS 2594.

Countermelody

Roll    on,   roll   on,   Roll    on, roll on.

## Two Different Sections

These pictures show you two things you will need to make carrot stew.

Can you find the signs that tell you this song has two different sections?

## Carrot Stew ⑤

Words and Music by Larry Groce

Ⓐ VERSE

D                          A₇         D

1. When - ev - er we have a   friend for lunch,

D                    G

There's just one thing to do. ___

D      A₇        G         D

We pick some ber-ries and catch some fish,

© 1976 Walt Disney Music Company. Used by permission.

And we make a car-rot stew.

**B** REFRAIN

Car-rot stew, car-rot stew,

It's our fav'-rite thing__ to do.

Get a pot and a car-rot or two,

And cook up a car-rot stew.

2. Nothing makes our tummies so full
   And keeps us happy too,
   As a great big pot or a little bitty bowl
   Or a spoonful of carrot stew. *Refrain*

3. So when you come to our little house,
   Bring a carrot if you have a few.
   We'll put it in a pot 'til it's nice and hot,
   And make some carrot stew. *Refrain*

Listen for two different sections in this piece for orchestra.

**5** *The Comedians.* . . . . . . . . . . . . . . . . **Kabalevsky**

# AB Form

Listen for the two sections in this song.

## Hop Up, My Ladies

American Folk Song

**A**  C                              C

1. Did you  ev-er  go  to  meet-ing,  Un-cle  Joe,  Un-cle  Joe?

C                              G₇

Did you  ev-er  go  to  meet-ing,  Un-cle  Joe? ___

C                              C

Did you  ev-er  go  to  meet-ing,  Un-cle  Joe,  Un-cle  Joe?

F              G₇      C

Don't  mind  the  weath-er,  so  the  wind  don't  blow.

Collected, adapted, and arranged by John A. Lomax and Alan Lomax TRO—© Copyright 1941 and renewed 1969 Ludlow Music, Inc., New York, NY. Used by permission.

**B**

C

Hop up, my la - dies,     three in a row,

C          G₇

Hop up, my la - dies  three in  a  row,

C

Hop up,  my  la - dies     three in  a  row,

F          G₇      C

Don't  mind  the  weath - er  so  the  wind don't blow.

2. Will your horse carry double, Uncle Joe, Uncle Joe?
   Don't mind the weather, so the wind don't blow. *Refrain*

3. Is your horse a single-footer, Uncle Joe, Uncle Joe?
   Don't mind the weather, so the wind don't blow. *Refrain*

**Do you find this rhythm pattern in section A
or in section B?**

Hop  up, my    la - dies

**Clap the pattern every time it comes in the song.**

## Shapes and Letters

**1.**

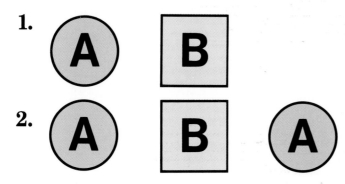

**2.**

Listen to the recording of "Hand Me Down." Which set of shapes and letters shows the form of the song?

# Hand Me Down

**Ⓐ** *Chorus*

Black Spiritual

Oh,   hand  me down,     Hand  me down,

Hand  me down  my sil-ver trum-pet, Ga-briel.

Hand me down, throw it down, An-y way to get  it down,

Hand  me down  my sil - ver trum-pet, Lord.

**Ⓑ** *Solo*

Oh,    Mo-ses had    a   lot  to do, —

© Copyright Edward B. Marks Music Company International copyright secured. ALL RIGHTS RESERVED. Used by permission.

**Chorus**

Hand me down my sil-ver trum-pet, Ga-briel,

**Solo**

When he led the chil-dren of Is-ra-el through,

**Chorus**

Hand me down my sil - ver trum - pet, Lord.

**(A) Chorus**

Oh, hand me down, Hand me down,

Hand me down my sil-ver trum-pet, Ga-briel.

Hand me down, throw it down, An-y way to get it down,

Hand me down my sil - ver trum - pet, Lord.

# The Sound of Voices

Follow the words of the poem *The Wind* as you
listen to the recording. Do you hear one voice?
Several voices?

## The Wind 🔘

I saw you toss the kites on high
And blow the birds about the sky;
And all around I heard you pass,
Like ladies' skirts across the grass—
   O wind, a-blowing all day long,
   O wind, that sings so loud a song!

I saw the different things you did,
But always you yourself you hid.
I felt you push, I heard you call,
I could not see yourself at all—
   O wind, a-blowing all day long,
   O wind, that sings so loud a song!

O you that are so strong and cold,
O blower, are you young or old?
Are you a beast of field and tree,
Or just a stronger child than me?
   O wind, a-blowing all day long,
   O wind, that sings so loud a song!

*Robert Louis Stevenson*

## One Voice—Many Voices

Listen for the solo parts in the recording of "Don't Stay Away." Sing along on the chorus parts when you can.

# Don't Stay Away 6

Black Spiritual

When you know the melody of "Don't Stay Away," try singing the solo parts. The class will sing the chorus parts.

# A Special Sound

Your voice has a special sound (tone color) whether you use it to whisper, speak, shout, or sing. No one else has a voice that sounds exactly like yours.

Listen for the voices on the recording of "Polly Wolly Doodle." Can you tell who is singing?

## Polly Wolly Doodle

American Folk Song

1. Oh, I went down South for to see my Sal,
2. Oh, my Sal, she is a ___ maid-en fair,

Sing-ing Pol-ly Wol-ly Doo-dle all the day;
Sing-ing Pol-ly Wol-ly Doo-dle all the day;

My — Sal, she is a — spunk-y gal,
With — curl-y eyes and — laugh-ing hair,

Sing-ing Pol-ly Wol-ly Doo-dle all the day.
Sing-ing Pol-ly Wol-ly Doo-dle all the day.

**REFRAIN**

Fare thee well, — fare thee well, — Fare thee well my fair-y fay, —

For I'm goin' to Loui-si-an-a, For to see my Su-sy-an-na,

Sing-ing Pol-ly Wol-ly Doo-dle all the day. ——

3. The partridge is a pretty bird,
   It has a speckled breast,
   It steals away the farmer's grain,
   And totes it to its nest! *Refrain*

4. The raccoon's tail is ringed around,
   The 'possum's tail is bare,
   The rabbit's got no tail at all,
   Just a little bitty bunch of hair! *Refrain*

# The Sounds of Instruments

Long ago, before Columbus discovered America,
people in Europe were listening to music played
on recorders.

Listen to the sound of recorders in this music. Can
you hear the instrument that plays the lowest tones
and the one that plays the very highest melody?

 **6** *Villancico* ........................ Encina

Do you recognize any of the instruments on this page? Which instrument do you think plays the lowest tones? Listening to this recording may help you decide.

 *The Special Sounds of Instruments*

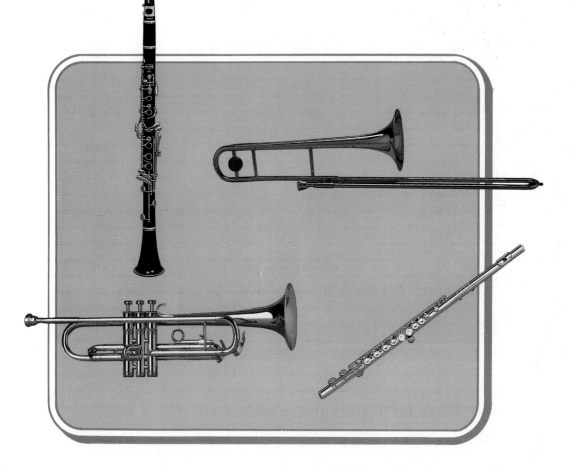

The instruments pictured on this page are called *wind instruments*. Can you tell why?

The music in this recording is played by a group of wind instruments.

 *Scherzo* . . . . . . . . . . . . . . . . . . . . . . . . . . . . . Bozza

# Ballet Music

*The Nutcracker Suite* by Tchaikovsky is music written for a ballet, a kind of dance that often tells a story.

One of the pieces Tchaikovsky used in this ballet music is called "Dance of the Reed Flutes." Can you guess what instrument you will hear first?

 "Dance of the Reed Flutes" from *The Nutcracker Suite* . . . . . . . . . . . . . . Tchaikovsky

# Melodies for Flute and Trumpet

Three flutes play the first melody.

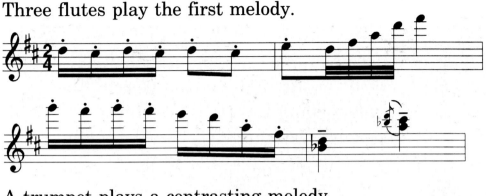

A trumpet plays a contrasting melody.

**Peter Illitch
Tchaikovsky**
(1840–1893)

Peter Illitch Tchaikovsky was born in Votkinsk, a little village in eastern Russia. From his earliest childhood Peter's main interest was music. But there were no concerts in Votkinsk, so most of Peter's music came from a music box that his father had brought from St. Petersburg. Peter would sit for hours listening to its tunes. As soon as he was big enough to sit at the piano, he began to make up tunes of his own.

Tchaikovsky composed a great deal of music. Today his beautiful melodies are heard in concert halls all over the world.

You will hear parts of seven pieces. Each time a number is called, decide whether the music moves in a meter of 2 or a meter of 3. Listen, then circle your answer on your worksheet.

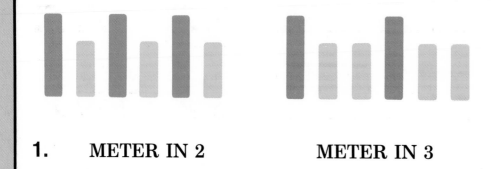

**1.**   METER IN 2          METER IN 3

**2.**   METER IN 2          METER IN 3

**3.**   METER IN 2          METER IN 3

**4.**   METER IN 2          METER IN 3

**5.**   METER IN 2          METER IN 3

**6.**   METER IN 2          METER IN 3

**7.**   METER IN 2          METER IN 3

Look in the right-hand column for the line of notes that matches the pattern of long and short lines in the left-hand column. On your worksheet, write its letter in the blank.

1. —    — — — —      A.

2. —    — — — — — —      B.

3. —    — — — — — —      C.

4. —    — — — — —      D.

5. —    — — — — — — —      E.

6. —    — — — — — —      F.

7. —    — — — — — —      G.

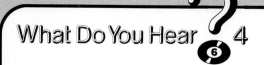 

You will hear seven melodies. Listen carefully for the ending of each melody. If the tones move upward at the end of the melody, circle the word UPWARD on your worksheet. If the tones move downward, circle the word DOWNWARD.

**1.**    UPWARD          DOWNWARD

**2.**    UPWARD          DOWNWARD

**3.**    UPWARD          DOWNWARD

**4.**    UPWARD          DOWNWARD

**5.**    UPWARD          DOWNWARD

**6.**    UPWARD          DOWNWARD

**7.**    UPWARD          DOWNWARD

Look at each example. If the notes repeat, write R
in the blank. If they move by step, write S in the
blank. If they leap, write L in the blank.

1. ____

2. ____

3. ____

4. ____

5. ____

6. ____

7. ____

8. ____

You will hear seven melodies. Each time a number is called, decide whether the tones in the melody move mostly by step, mostly by leap, or mostly by repeated tones. Listen, then circle your answer on your worksheet.

| 1. | STEP | LEAP | REPEAT |
|----|------|------|--------|
| 2. | STEP | LEAP | REPEAT |
| 3. | STEP | LEAP | REPEAT |
| 4. | STEP | LEAP | REPEAT |
| 5. | STEP | LEAP | REPEAT |
| 6. | STEP | LEAP | REPEAT |
| 7. | STEP | LEAP | REPEAT |

## What Do You Hear 6 — Phrases

You will hear seven musical examples. Each example has two phrases. When a number is called, listen to both phrases. If the phrases are exactly alike, circle the word SAME on your worksheet. If the phrases are not alike, circle the word DIFFERENT. Listen, then circle your answer.

1. SAME DIFFERENT

2. SAME DIFFERENT

3. SAME DIFFERENT

4. SAME DIFFERENT

5. SAME DIFFERENT

6. SAME DIFFERENT

7. SAME DIFFERENT

## A. What is the form shown in each example below?

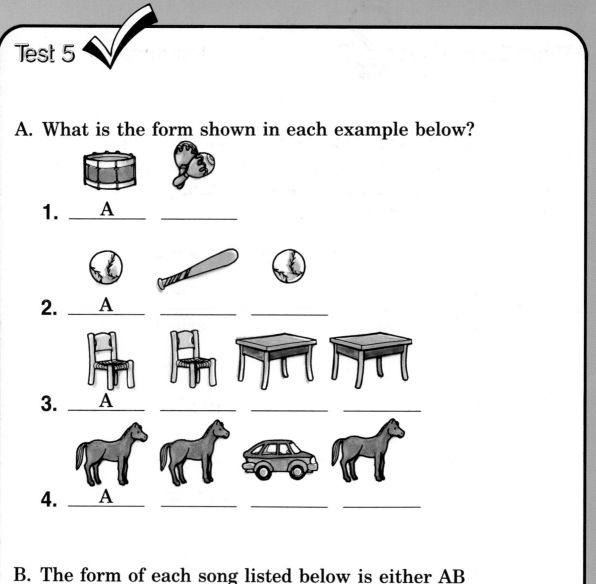

1. ___A___  _____

2. ___A___  _____  _____

3. ___A___  _____  _____  _____

4. ___A___  _____  _____  _____

## B. The form of each song listed below is either AB or ABA. Look through the music and on your worksheet, write the name of the form in the blank.

1. The Dummy Line ____

2. Stodala Pumpa ____

3. I'd 've Baked a Cake ____

4. Boil Them Cabbage Down ____

5. Nine Red Horsemen ____

6. Hand Me Down ____

You will hear six melodies. Each melody is played by a wind instrument. When a number is called, decide which instrument is playing. Listen, then circle your answer on your worksheet.

**1.**  recorder

trumpet

clarinet

trombone

flute

**2.**  recorder

trumpet

clarinet

trombone

flute

**3.**  recorder

trumpet

clarinet

trombone

flute

**4.**  recorder

trumpet

clarinet

trombone

flute

**5.**  recorder

trumpet

clarinet

trombone

flute

**6.**  recorder

trumpet

clarinet

trombone

flute

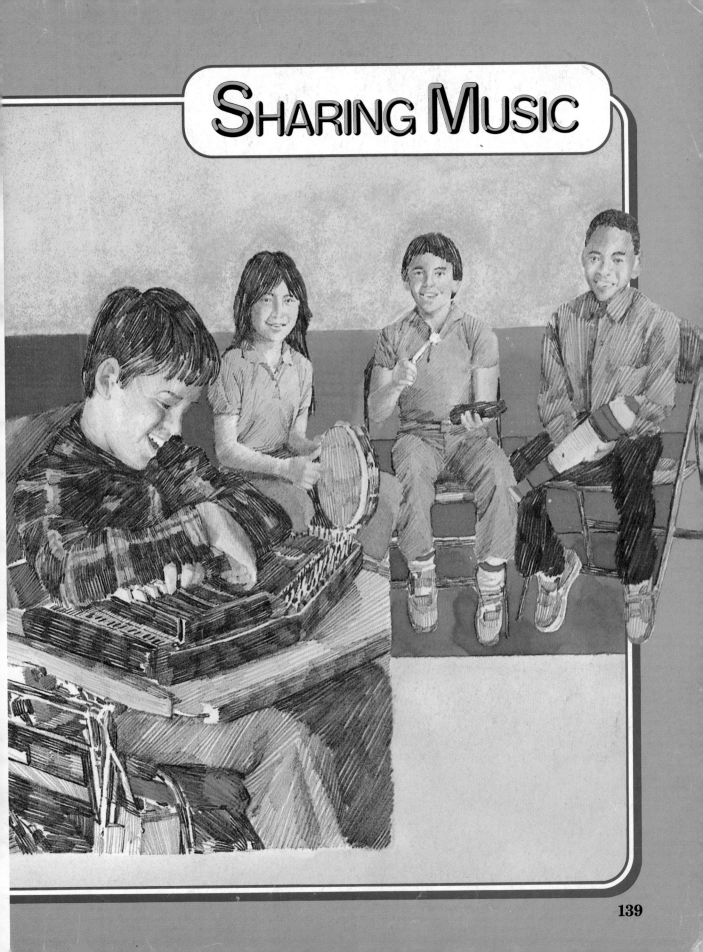

# Friends Sing Together

One of the nicest things in life is having friends.
Friends who help each other are special.

Are you a special friend?

## The Friendship Song

Words and Music by Philip Balsam and Dennis Lee

Re-mem-ber when _ now and then _ ev-'ry-thing _ went wrong,

And then our friends _ would sing the friend-ship song, _____

You and I ___ would near-ly cry _ to know their love _ was strong,

And by and by ___ we'd start to sing _ a - long. _____

We'd sing, "Try a lit-tle long-er for your friend. _____

Try a lit-tle strong-er for your friend." _____

© 1983 Henson Associates, Inc. Administered by Muppet Music, Inc. (ASCAP) International Copyright Secured. ALL RIGHTS RESERVED. Used by permission.

You work all night, — work all day, —

You just can't keep those wor-ried blues a-way. —————

Try a lit-tle long-er for your friend. ———

Try a lit-tle strong-er for your friend. ———

## An Add-On Song

This is a special kind of song. To find out why, listen to the recording.

# Green Leaves Grew All Around

Folk Song from England

1. All in __ a __ wood there grew a tree,
2. And on __ this __ tree there grew a limb,

The fin - est __ tree you ev - er did see;
The fin - est __ limb you ev - er did see;

The tree was in the wood,
The limb was on the tree,   The tree was in the wood,

And the green leaves grew all a - round, a-round, a-round,

And the green leaves grew all a - round.

*Repeat for additional lines in verses 3–8.

3. And on this limb there was a branch,
   The finest branch you ever did see;
   The branch was on the limb,
   The limb was on the tree,
   The tree was in the wood,
   And the green leaves grew . . .

4. And on this branch there was a nest, . . .

5. And in this nest there was an egg, . . .

6. And in this egg there was a bird, . . .

7. And on this bird there was a wing, . . .

8. And on this wing there was a feather, . . .

# King of the Cornfield

Standing guard over a cornfield is a lonely job!

## The Tired Scarecrow

Traditional

1. Stand - ing   there,      a   tir - ed scare - crow,

Does - n't   care        how hard   the wind   blows,

Win - ter's   chill   is      on      the   hill,   and the

Scare - crow   knows   it's      au - tumn. _____

2.  He stood guard, king of the cornfield,
    Working hard, there in the cornfield,
    Did his best, now he can rest
    Till the planting time next year.

Bells

# Dynamics—Soft or Loud

Listen to the recording of "Little Boy of the Sheep."
Then point to the word at the top of the page that
describes how the song is sung.

## Little Boy of the Sheep

Folk Song from the Hebrides Islands    English Words by Alice Firgau

**A** Sing me a song, pipe me a tune,

Guard the sheep well, O shep - herd boy.

**B** Keep - ing the sheep all day, watch - ing they do not stray,

O - ver the hill - side, O shep - herd boy.

From FOLKSONGS AND FOLKLORE OF THE SOUTH UIST, by J. L. Campbell. © 1955 by Routledge & Kegan Paul, Ltd.

Listen for the instrument that pipes a tune
in this music.

*Siciliana* . . . . . . . . . . . . . . . . . . . . . . . . . . . . Bach

## A Story with Music

This song is about a drummer boy. To find out what happens to him, follow the words as you listen to the recording.

# Three Drummer Boys

French Folk Song     English Version by Margaret Marks

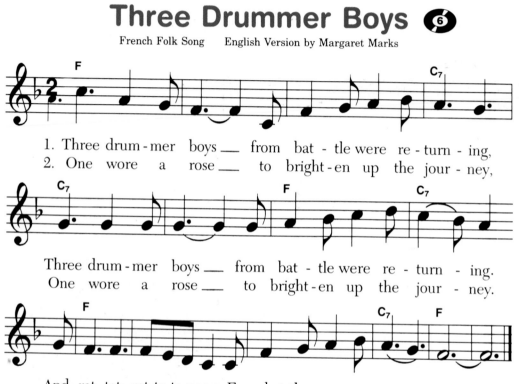

1. Three drum-mer boys __ from bat - tle were re - turn - ing,
2. One wore a rose __ to bright-en up the jour - ney,

Three drum-mer boys __ from bat - tle were re - turn - ing.
One wore a rose __ to bright-en up the jour - ney.

And rat, tat, rat-ta-ta poom, From bat-tle were re - turn - ing. __
And rat, tat, rat-ta-ta poom, To bright-en up the jour - ney. __

3. Princess Marie was watching from her tower,

4. "Sweet drummer boy, will you give me your flower?"

5. "Give me your heart and give it to no other,"

6. "Sweet drummer boy, you'll have to ask my father,"

7. "O gracious King, will you give me your daughter?"

8. "No drummer boy, you have no gold to court her,"

9. "Three ships have I a-sailing on the water,"

10. "One's filled with gold, the other filled with treasure,"

11. "As for the third, I keep it for my pleasure,"

12. "Sweet drummer boy, then you may wed my daughter,"

13. "O gracious King, I wish to thank you kindly,"

14. "But in my land, we do not wed so blindly,"

## Drummer-Boy Band

Which part will you play in the Drummer-Boy Band?

# The Firebird

The story that Igor Stravinsky tells in his ballet *The Firebird* is about the adventures of Prince Ivan, hero of many Russian folktales, and a mysterious bird with flaming feathers. In one part of the story, the firebird lulls a beautiful princess into a magic sleep to protect her from an evil king. Here is the music from that part of the story.

**"Berceuse"** from *Firebird Suite* . . **Stravinsky**

Here is a little pattern that you hear all through the music.

Listen for this sleepy bassoon melody near the beginning of the piece.

**Igor Stravinsky**
(1882–1971)

Igor Stravinsky was born in Russia. His father was a famous singer at the Russian Imperial Opera. Igor often went to opera rehearsals with his father and learned to love the musical theater when he was still a young boy.

During his lifetime Stravinsky composed many pieces for the musical theater. In addition to *The Firebird*, he wrote a ballet about a puppet called *Petrouchka* and one called *The Soldier's Tale*.

## A Cradle Song

How would you sing a lullaby? Which list of words
describes how a lullaby should be sung?

| | |
|---|---|
| soft | jerky |
| quiet | fast |
| gentle | loud |

# Now Sleep, Little Fellow
## (Dormite, niñito)

Folk Song from El Salvador

Now sleep, lit-tle fel - low,  Sleep safe in your cra - dle;
*Dor-mi - te, ni - ñi - to,*  *No llo - res, chi -qui - to,*

The shad-ows of ev - 'ning  Creep o - ver the gar - den,
*Ven-drán an-ge - li - tos,*  *Las som-bras de no - che,*

The rays of the moon -light,  Like fine threads of sil - ver,
*Ray - i -tos de pla - ta,*  *Ray - i - tos de pla - ta,*

Will shine on the ba - by  A - sleep in his cra - dle.
*A - lum-bran a mi ni - ño,*  *Que es -ta en la cu - na.*

The morn-ing will come soon
*Ray - i - tos del    sol, ___*

With blue sky and sun - shine,
*El   cie - lo    a - zul ___*

The birds will a - wak - en
*De - jan   de dor - mir ___*

To  sing their sweet song.
*Y em - pie - zan  a vi - vir,*

So sleep, lit - tle   fel - low,
*Dor - mi - te, ni - ñi - to,*

While stars in   the   dark skies
*Con    o - jus de dia - man - tes,*

Are twink - ling a - bove   you
*Es - tre - llas bri - llan - tes,*

like flow - ers of  heav - en.
*Flo - ri - do el   cie - lo.*

# Follow the Phrase Lines

Follow the phrase lines marked over the music as you listen to "Garden Song." Are all the phrases the same length? Are some of the phrases short and others long?

## Garden Song ⑦

Words and Music by David Mallett

1. Inch by inch, row by row, —
2. Pull - in' weeds and pick - in' stones, —

Gon - na make this gar - den grow, —
Man is made of dreams and bones, —

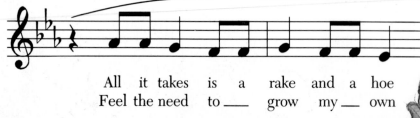

All it takes is a rake and a hoe
Feel the need to — grow my — own

© Copyright 1975/1978 CHERRY LANE MUSIC PUBLISHING CO., INC. All Rights Reserved. Used by permission.

and   a piece of fer-tile   ground. ____
'cause the time is close at   hand. ____

Inch   by   inch,   row by   row, __
Grain  for  grain,  sun and  rain __

Some-one bless  the   seeds I   sow,
Find  my   way  in   na-ture's chain,

Some-one warm them   from  be-low __
Tune  my  bod-y    and  my  brain __

'til   the   rain comes tum-bl-ing   down.
to   the   mu-sic  from __ the   land.

3. Plant your rows straight and strong,
Temper them with prayer and song,
Mother Earth will make you strong
if you give her love and care.
Old crow watching hungrily
From his perch in yonder tree,
In my garden I'm as free
as that feathered thief up there.

# Melody and Countermelody

Trace the rise and fall of this melody in the air. Pretend you are painting an autumn scene with a big paintbrush.

## Autumn

English Folk Song

1. Au - tumn comes, the sum - mer is past,
2. Au - tumn comes, but let us be glad,

Win - ter will come too soon. _____
Sing - ing an au - tumn tune. _____

Stars will shine clear - er, skies seem near - er,
Hearts will be light - er, nights be bright - er,

Un - der the Har - vest Moon. _____
Un - der the Har - vest Moon. _____

Bells

R.H.

L.H.

R.H.

L.H.

# Autumn's Countermelody

Countermelody

1. Au - tumn comes, the sum - mer is past,
2. Au - tumn comes, but let us be glad,

Win - ter will come too __ soon. _____
Sing - ing an au - tumn _ tune. _____

Stars will shine clear - er, skies seem near - er,
Hearts will be light - er, nights be bright - er,

Un - der the Har - vest Moon. _____
Un - der the Har - vest Moon. _____

## Autumn Woods

I like the woods
    In autumn
When dry leaves hide the ground,
When the trees are bare
And the wind sweeps by
With a lonesome rushing sound.

I can rustle the leaves
    In autumn
And I can make a bed
In the thick dry leaves
That have fallen
From the bare trees
Overhead.

*James S. Tippett*

# Singing a Story

A song that tells a story is called a *ballad*. Read the words of this ballad. What kind of story does it tell?

## A Little Ship

French Folk Song    English Version by Margaret Marks

1. A lit - tle    ship once went a - sail - ing,

A lit - tle    ship once went a - sail - ing,

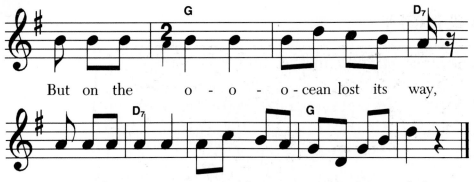

But on the o - o - o-cean lost its way,

But on the o - o - o-cean lost its way, *O-hé, o - hé!*

2. And after weeks and weeks of sailing *(2 times)*
   There were no ra-ra-rations left one day. *(2 times)*
   *Ohé, ohé!*

3. The crew drew lots to choose the sailor
   Whom they should ea-ea-eat for *déjeuner.*

4. The choice fell on the youngest sailor,
   He was the one, one, one they would *sauté.*

5. And while they argued how to serve him,
   With lemon sau-sau-sauce or *Bordelaise,*

6. A hundred thousand flying fishes
   Jumped on the de-de-deck and there they lay.

7. And so the sailors ate the fishes.
   The boy was sa-sa-saved, oh happy day!

8. If you've enjoyed this little ditty
   We'll sing it o-o-over right away.

## A Part for Bells

Play this part to accompany "A Little Ship." You will
need two bells—the G bell and the D bell.

# Flower Song from China

Play a sound on a ringing instrument for each X.

## The Jasmine Flower 7

Folk Song from China    English Words Adapted by Julia Bingham

1. See — this   branch — of — sweet - est — flow'rs,
2. Take — this   branch — of — jas - mine — flow'rs,

Plucked — at   morn — from — dew - y — bow'rs;
Plucked — at   morn — from — dew - y — bow'rs;

Sent   with   love — to   greet   me,
Given   with   love — to   greet   you,

Breath - ing   friend - ship   sweet.
Breath - ing   friend - ship   sweet.

## Add a Part

158

## Make a Wish

What would you like to find
at the end of a rainbow?

# Look to the Rainbow

from *Finian's Rainbow*

Words by E. Y. Harburg     Music by Burton Lane

Look, look, look to the rain - bow.

Fol - low it o - ver the hill ___ and stream.

Look, look, look to the rain - bow.

Fol - low the fel - low who fol - lows a dream.

Fol - low the fel - low, Fol - low the fel - low,

Fol - low the fel - low who fol - lows a dream.

Copyright © 1947 by Chappell & Co., Inc. Copyright renewed. International copyright secured. ALL RIGHTS RESERVED. Used by permission.

# A Song for All Seasons

You can sing this beautiful song at any time of the year.

## May Day Carol

English Folk Song

*Gently*

1. The moon shines bright, The stars give light,
2. A branch of May I bring to you

A lit - tle be - fore 'tis day.
As at ___ the door I stand.

Our Heav - en - ly Fa - ther, He called to us
'Tis but ___ a sprout well ___ bud - ded out,

And bid us to wake and pray.
The work of ___ our Lord's hands.

A - wake, a - wake, O pret - ty, pret - ty maid,
My song is done, I must ___ be ___ gone,

| Out | of | your | drow - sy | dream. |
| No | long - er | can | I | stay. |

(Chord: C)

| And | step | in - to | your | dair - y | be - low |
| God | bless | you | all, | both | great _ | and small, |

(Chords: E₇ · A MIN · G₇ · C)

| And | fetch | me | a | bowl | of | cream. |
| And | send | you | a | joy - ful | May. |

(Chords: F · C)

## There Is but One May

There is but one May in the year,
   And sometimes May is wet and cold;
There is but one May in the year
   Before the year grows old.

Yet though it be the chilliest May,
   With least of sun and most of showers,
Its wind and dew, its night and day,
   Bring up the flowers.

*Christina Georgina Rossetti*

# A Musical Greeting

This song would be a good one to sing for United Nations Day. Can you tell why?

## We Come to Greet You in Peace
### (Hevenu Shalom Aleichem)

Hebrew Folk Song

Play a tambourine accompaniment
all through the song.

# Song Without Words

Some songs have no words—only syllables like *tra la la.* The *bims, boms,* and *biris* in this song are fun to sing. Sing along with the recording when you can.

## Bim Bom

Jewish Folk Song

# Music for Harpsichord

The instrument shown in the picture above is called a *harpsichord*. You will find a picture of one of the harpsichord's relatives on page 100 in your music book. Look at the pictures of the two instruments. Can you see that the harpsichord and the piano are related?

Here is some harpsichord music by Handel. Can you hear that the sound of the harpsichord is different from the sound of the piano?

   *The Harmonious Blacksmith*........Handel

Here is the melody, or theme, that you hear at
the beginning of *The Harmonious Blacksmith*.
You might try following the music as you listen
to the recording again.

**George Frideric Handel**
(1685–1759)

George Frideric Handel was born in the small German village of Halle. When he was still a child, George decided that he would be a musician when he grew up.

Handel went on to become one of the greatest composers of all times. During his lifetime he wrote music to be sung and music for all kinds of instruments, including the well-known harpsichord piece *The Harmonious Blacksmith*.

Read the sentences below. On your worksheet,
write T in the blank if the sentence is true. Write
F in the blank if the sentence is false.

1. Recognizing like phrases makes a song easier
to learn. _____

2. An ostinato is a pattern that is repeated over
and over again. _____

3. All songs should be sung at the same tempo. _____

4. Cymbals and drums are good instruments to
use with a marching song. _____

5. The words of a song often give a clue as to
how the song should be sung. _____

6. A lullaby should be sung loud and fast. _____

7. A ballad is a song that tells a story. _____

8. The term *dynamics* means the loudness and
softness of sound. _____

9. A coda comes at the end of a piece. _____

10. This is a repeat sign— :‖ . _____

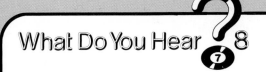
You will hear four sets of pieces. In each set, one piece is in a slow tempo, the other in a fast tempo. Listen to both pieces, decide which is slow and which is fast, then circle your answers on your worksheet.

**1.**  First piece      SLOW      FAST

     Second piece      SLOW      FAST

**2.**  First piece      SLOW      FAST

     Second piece      SLOW      FAST

**3.**  First piece      SLOW      FAST

     Second piece      SLOW      FAST

**4.**  First piece      SLOW      FAST

     Second piece      SLOW      FAST

MUSEUM OF
COMMUNICATION

GUIDE

GUIDE

KETTI KNIPPER

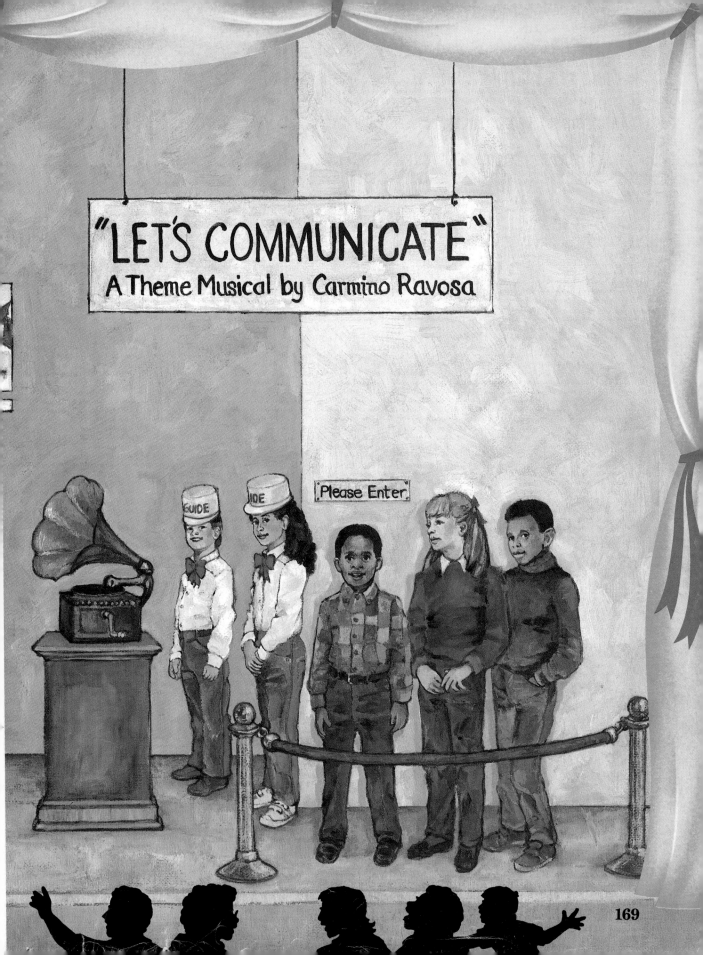

169

**Guide 1:** Welcome to The (name) Museum of Communication and to our show, "Let's Communicate." Members of Miss (name) class will be your guides.

# Step Right This Way

Words and Music by Carmino Ravosa

1.–3. Step right this way. ___ Step right this way. ___ The

*Last time to Coda*

tour is start-ing, ___ so step right this way. ___ Step right this way. ___

1. Keep to-geth - er and pay at - ten - tion and
2.  No push - ing and  no rush - ing and
3. You'll en - joy ___ ev - 'ry min - ute of ___ it, yes

step live - ly, oh did I men - tion to
no talk - ing, and  no touch - ing, so
we know ___ that you're gon - na love ___ it, so

*Coda*

Step right this way!

**Guide 2:** What is communication?

**Guide 3:** Communication is an exchange of feelings, thoughts, or information.

**Guide 4:** When you talk with your mother or father, you are communicating with spoken words. When you write a letter, you are communicating with written words.

**Guide 5:** People are the only creatures on earth who can express thoughts in words.

**Guide 6:** Some scientists think that people began to speak about 34,000 years ago. And before people began to talk, they probably used gestures to communicate.

**Guide 7:** We still use gestures. When we shake hands, we are saying "Hello" without making a sound.

**Guide 8:** In China, people bow. Laplanders rub noses. Latin American men embrace. Soldiers salute.

**Guide 9:** And clowns! They always talk without saying a word.

# He's a Clown

Words and Music by Carmino Ravosa

He's a clown, he's a clown, he's a clown. He's the
clown, he's a clown, he's a clown. When he

fun - ni - est man in the town. From his
trips and he falls on the ground. He's not

head to his toe, we all know, He's a clown._____ He's a
play - ing a part, in his heart, He's a

clown.          He'd rath - er be a clown than the Pres - i - dent.

He'd rath - er be a clown than a king.                He'd

rath-er be a clown than an as-tro-naut, Or an-y oth-er thing.

He's a clown, he's a clown, he's a clown. Seems he

does ev-'ry-thing up-side down, He's not play-ing a part, in his heart,

He's a clown.___ He's a clown, he's a clown. I'm a clown! He's a clown!

**Guide 10:** There are many ways to communicate. Signs communicate: No Smoking, Deer Crossing, Watch Out for Children.

**Guide 11:** And how about *sound* as a way of communicating? We have fire alarms and police whistles—even doorbells.

**Guide 12:** People talk about how great it would be if there was a language that everyone in the world could understand. Well, in a way, we have such a language— music! But you have to sing it or play it.

# Music Is Not Music Unless You Sing It 7

Words and Music by Carmino Ravosa

1. Mu - sic is not mu - sic un - less you sing it. ___
2. Mu - sic is not mu - sic un - less you play it. ___

Mu - sic is not mu - sic un - less you do. do.

It's just a lot of lit - tle fly - specks on a pa - per, ___ a

lot of lit - tle dots that are on a sheet. ___ It

does - n't mean a thing un - less you sing ___ it, and

*D.C. Verse 1 al Fine*

bring it a beat, two, three, four, five, six, sev'n, eight!

Communication took a big step forward when the printing press was invented. What would we do today without our newspapers?

## Extra, Extra

Words and Music by Carmino Ravosa

**Guide 14:** Thomas Edison had to try and try again before he got the phonograph to work.

# If at First You Don't Succeed

Words and Music by Carmino Ravosa

If at first you don't suc-ceed, Try and try a - gain.

If at first you don't suc-ceed, Try and try a - gain,

And you will find, If you've got the mind,
And you will see, Take ___ it from me.

To do it, go through it, you will.
Be - gin it, you'll win it, you'll see.

If at first you don't suc-ceed, Try and try a - gain.

If at first you don't suc-ceed, Try and try a - gain!

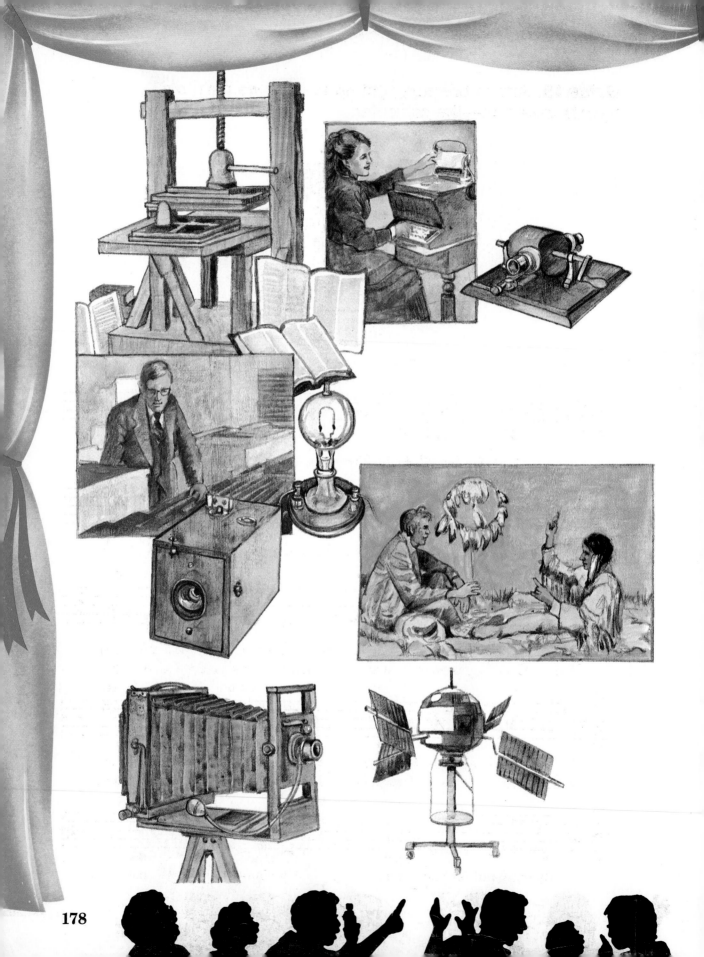

**Guide 15:** And to bring us right up to date, we have our favorite invention—the computer.

# My Computer and Me

Words and Music by Carmino Ravosa

My com-put-er and me, My com-put-er and me,

We're as hap-py can be, My com-put-er and me.

We can add, sub-tract, or mul-ti-ply, di-vide, as you can see.
In ___ play-ing games it does-n't cheat, get bored and want to go.

We can read or write or draw or paint or write a sym-pho-ny.
It ___ doesn't get mad or jeal-ous ___ like some-one that I know.

My com-put-er and me, My com-put-er and me.

**Guide 16:** We've come a long way in communications—or have we? A smile still communicates more than any word. Do you know that a smile is the shortest distance between two people?

# The Shortest Distance Between Two People

Words and Music by Carmino Ravosa

The short-est dis-tance be-tween two peo-ple is a smile.

The short-est dis-tance be-tween two peo-ple is a smile.

The short-est dis-tance, The path of least re-sist-ance,

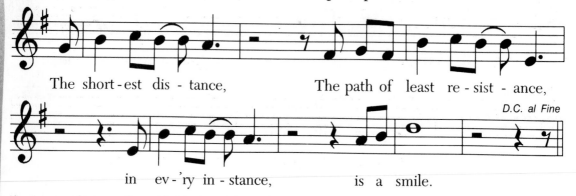

in ev-'ry in-stance, is a smile.

**Guide 17:** When is the last time you said "Thank you" to your mother or father or your teacher or your best friend—said "Thank you for being you"?

# Thank You for Being You

Words and Music by Carmino Ravosa

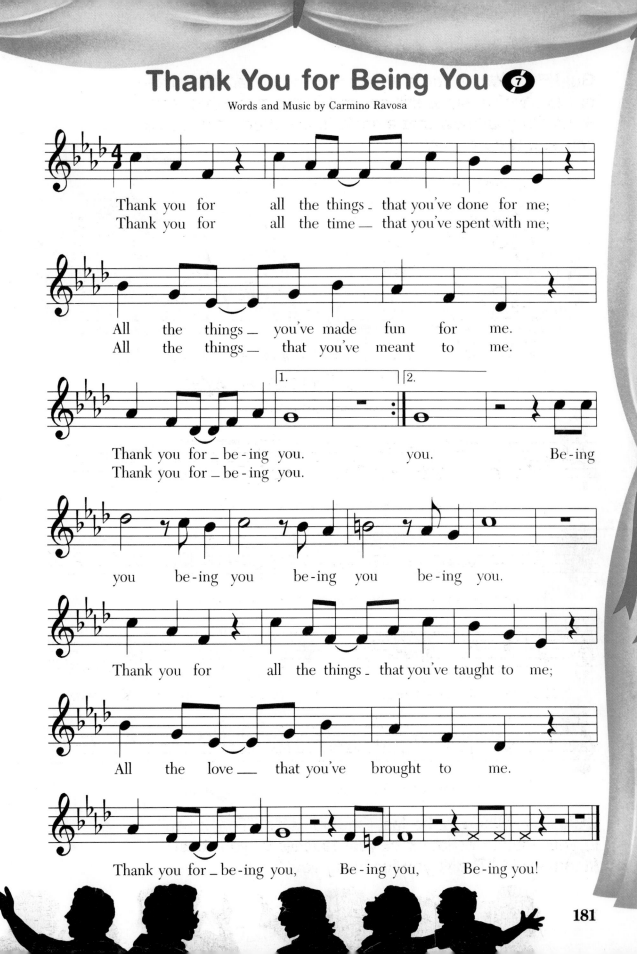

Thank you for all the things that you've done for me;
Thank you for all the time that you've spent with me;

All the things you've made fun for me.
All the things that you've meant to me.

Thank you for being you.                you.                Be-ing
Thank you for being you.

you    be-ing you    be-ing you    be-ing you.

Thank you for all the things that you've taught to me;

All the love that you've brought to me.

Thank you for being you,    Be-ing you,    Be-ing you!

181

**Guide 18:** No matter how well we get along with someone near to us, we've got to get along with everybody else in the world.

**Guide 19:** So, let's communicate. We've got to get together before it's too late.

# Let's Communicate

Words and Music by Carmino Ravosa

Let's com - mun - i - cate, _ let's com - mun - i - cate. _ We've

got to get to - geth - er be - fore it's too late. _ Let's com -

mun - i - cate, _ Let's com - mun - i - cate, _ We've

got to get to - geth - er and we just can't wait. _

We should try to get a - long with each oth - er, We've

got to try to un-der-stand one an-oth-er.

Coda

Let's com-mun-i-cate, _ Let's com-mun-i-cate, _ We've

slower

got to get to-geth-er and we just can't wait. _

| Jan | 1 2 3 4 5 6 | Jul | 1 2 3 4 5 6 |
|-----|-------------|-----|-------------|
| | 7 8 9 10 11 12 13 14 15 | | 7 8 9 10 11 12 13 14 15 |
| | 16 17 18 19 20 21 22 23 24 | | 16 17 18 19 20 21 22 23 24 |
| | 25 26 27 28 29 30 31 | | 25 26 27 28 29 30 31 |

| Feb | 1 2 3 4 5 6 | Aug | 1 2 3 4 5 6 |
|-----|-------------|-----|-------------|
| | 7 8 9 10 11 12 13 14 15 | | 7 8 9 10 11 12 13 14 15 |
| | 16 17 18 19 20 21 22 23 24 | | 16 17 18 19 20 21 22 23 24 |
| | 25 26 27 28 | | 25 26 27 28 29 30 31 |

| Mar | 1 2 3 4 5 6 | Sep | 1 2 3 4 5 6 |
|-----|-------------|-----|-------------|
| | 7 8 9 10 11 12 13 14 15 | | 7 8 9 10 11 12 13 14 15 |
| | 16 17 18 19 20 21 22 23 24 | | 16 17 18 19 20 21 22 23 24 |
| | 25 26 27 28 29 30 31 | | 25 26 27 28 29 30 |

| Apr | 1 2 3 4 5 6 | Oct | 1 2 3 4 5 6 |
|-----|-------------|-----|-------------|
| | 7 8 9 10 11 12 13 14 15 | | 7 8 9 10 11 12 13 14 15 |
| | 16 17 18 19 20 21 22 23 24 | | 16 17 18 19 20 21 22 23 24 |
| | 25 26 27 28 29 30 | | 25 26 27 28 29 30 31 |

| May | 1 2 3 4 5 6 | Nov | 1 2 3 4 5 6 |
|-----|-------------|-----|-------------|
| | 7 8 9 10 11 12 13 14 15 | | 7 8 9 10 11 12 13 14 15 |
| | 16 17 18 19 20 21 22 23 24 | | 16 17 18 19 20 21 22 23 24 |
| | 25 26 27 28 29 30 | | 25 26 27 28 29 30 |

| Jun | 1 2 3 4 5 6 | Dec | 1 2 3 4 5 6 |
|-----|-------------|-----|-------------|
| | 7 8 9 10 11 12 13 14 15 | | 7 8 9 10 11 12 13 14 15 |
| | 16 17 18 19 20 21 22 23 24 | | 16 17 18 19 20 21 22 23 24 |
| | 25 26 27 28 29 30 | | 25 26 27 28 29 30 31 |

184

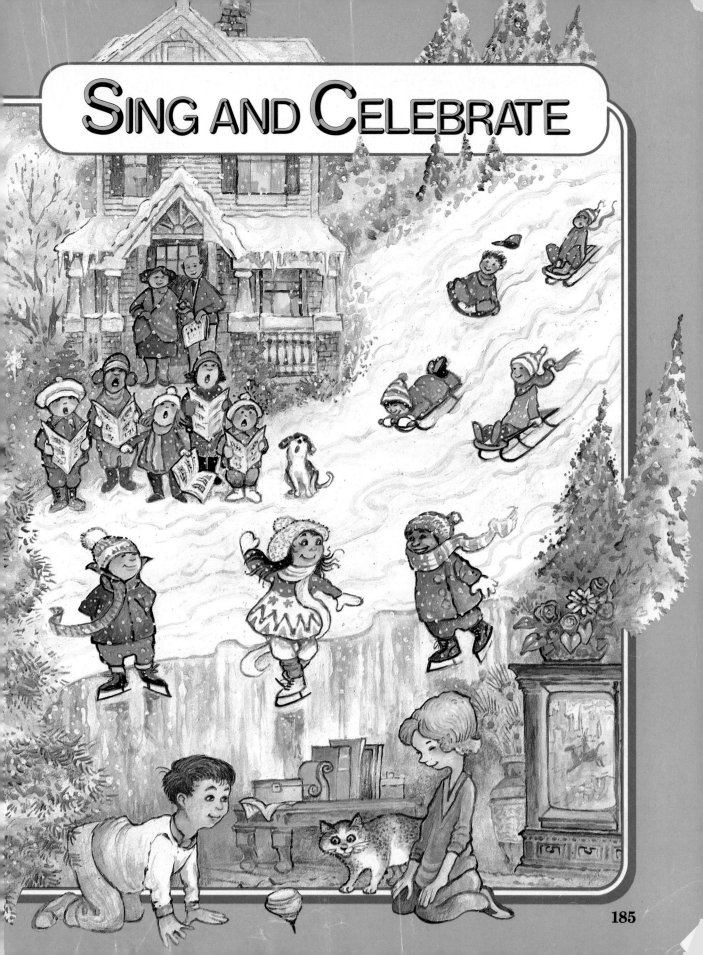

# SING AND CELEBRATE

# Our National Anthem

What should you do when our national anthem is sung or played?

## The Star-Spangled Banner

Words by Francis Scott Key    Music by John Stafford Smith

Oh, — say! can you see, by the dawn's ear - ly light,

What so proud - ly we hailed at the twi-light's last gleam-ing,

Whose broad stripes and bright stars, through the per - il - ous fight,

O'er the ram - parts we watched were so gal - lant - ly stream-ing?

And the rock - ets' red glare, the bombs burst-ing in air,

Gave proof through the night that our flag was still there.

Oh,   say, does  that _ Star-Span-gled  Ban-ner _ yet _ wave _

O'er the   land __ of the free   and the home  of the   brave.

National holidays are often celebrated with fireworks. Listen for the "fireworks" in this piece. What makes the music so exciting?

*Fireworks*........................Stravinsky

Here is how a poet describes fireworks.

## Fireworks

They rise like sudden fiery flowers
  That burst upon the night,
Then fall to earth in burning showers
  Of crimson, blue, and white.

Like buds too wonderful to name,
  Each miracle unfolds,
And catherine-wheels begin to flame
  Like whirling marigolds.

Rockets and roman candles make
  An orchard of the sky,
Whence magic trees their petals shake
  Upon each gazing eye.

*James Reeves*

# Let Freedom Ring

What do you think of when you read the words
*liberty* and *freedom*? Think about those words when
you sing this song.

## America

Traditional Melody    Words by Samuel Francis Smith

My coun-try! 'tis of thee, Sweet land of lib-er-ty,

Of thee I sing; Land where my fa-thers died,

Land of the Pil-grims' pride, From ev-'ry — moun-tain-side

Let — free-dom ring!

Our fathers' God, to Thee, Author of liberty,
To Thee we sing; Long may our land be bright
With freedom's holy light; Protect us by Thy might,
Great God, our King!

# From Sea to Shining Sea

Some of the words in this song paint a picture of our land. Can you paint a picture that would show America, the beautiful?

## America, the Beautiful

Words by Katharine Lee Bates    Music by Samuel A. Ward

1. O beau - ti - ful for spa - cious skies, For am - ber waves of grain,
2. O beau - ti - ful for pa - triot dream That sees be - yond the years

For pur - ple moun - tain maj - es - ties A - bove the fruit - ed plain!
Thine al - a - bas - ter cit - ies gleam, Un - dimmed by hu - man tears!

A - mer - i - ca! A - mer - i - ca! God shed His grace on thee,

And crown thy good with broth - er - hood From sea to shin - ing sea!

# An Old Favorite

"Yankee Doodle" is a favorite song of boys and girls
all over America. Many verses have been written for
the tune. Here are the words that you may know best.

Yankee Doodle came to town
Riding on a pony,
Stuck a feather in his cap
And called it macaroni.

## Yankee Doodle

Traditional     Words by Dr. Richard Shuckburgh

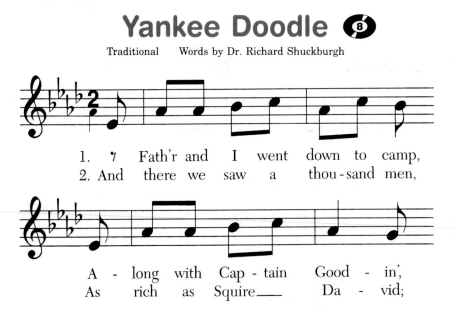

1. 𝄽 Fath'r and I went down to camp,
2. And there we saw a thou-sand men,

A - long with Cap - tain Good - in',
As rich as Squire___ Da - vid;

And there we saw the men and boys
And what they wast-ed ev-'ry day,

As thick as hast-y pud-din'.
I wish it could be sav-ed.

**REFRAIN**

Yan-kee Doo-dle, keep it up, Yan-kee Doo-dle dan-dy,

Mind the mu-sic and the step And with the girls be hand-y.

3. And there was Captain Washington
Upon a slapping stallion,
A-giving orders to his men;
I guess there was a million.

## Parts for Percussion

Which percussion part will you play? Which instrument
will you use to accompany this marching song?

# Sound of Halloween

Listen for the Halloween sounds that accompany the voices on the recording of "The Ghost of John."

## The Ghost of John

Words and Music by Martha Grubb

I
Have you seen the ghost of John?

II
Long white bones with the skin all gone, _____

Oo, Oo, _____

Would-n't it be chil-ly with no skin on!

Play your own accompaniment for "The Ghost of John." Which pattern will you choose?

**Bells**

Play 4 times.

**Guiro**

Play 4 times.

# Halloween Night

Read the words of this song as a poem. Then think of
ways to use your singing voice to make the song exciting.

## Hallowe'en

Words by Harry Behn     Music by Milton Kaye

To - night is the night when dead leaves fly

Like witch - es on switch - es a - cross the sky.

When elf and sprite flit through the night on a

moon - y sheen, It's Hal - low - e'en.

Words from THE LITTLE HILL, Poems & Pictures by Harry Behn. Copyright 1949 by Harry Behn. © renewed 1977 by Alice L. Behn. Used by permission of Marian Reiner.

Try this accompaniment for guiro and voices.
Then make up an accompaniment of your own.

Guiro

Voices

Oooh.          Oooh.

193

# Halloween Cat

The first line of this song tells you that an old black cat hates Halloween. The last line tells you why.

## My Old Black Cat Hates Halloween

Words and Music by Linda Williams

My old black cat hates Hal - low - een,

He shakes and quakes and cries.

He should be good on Hal - low - een,

But much to my sur - prise,

He stays in bed and hides his head,

Now, why does he do that?

© 1986 SUNDANCE MUSIC

194

"Me - ow," he says, "Me - ow," he says,

"I'm just a scare - dy cat!"

## Halloween Indignation Meeting

A sulky witch
  and a surly cat
And a scowly owl
  and a skeleton sat
With a grouchy ghost
  and a waspish bat,
And angrily snarled
  and chewed the fat.

It seems they were
  all upset and riled
That they couldn't frighten
  the Modern Child,
Who was much too knowing
  and much too wild
And considered Hallowe'en
  spooks too mild.

Said the witch, "They call this
  the *human* race.
Yet the kiddies inhabit
  Outer Space;
They bob for comets,
  and eat ice cream
From flying saucers,
  to get up steam!"

"I'm a shade of my former self,"
  said the skeleton.
"I shiver and shake
  like so much gelatine,
Indeed I'm a pitiful
  sight to see—
I'm scareder of *kids*
  than they are of *me!*"

*Margaret Fishback*

# Harvest Home

# Come, Ye Thankful People, Come

Words by Henry Alford    Music by George J. Elvey

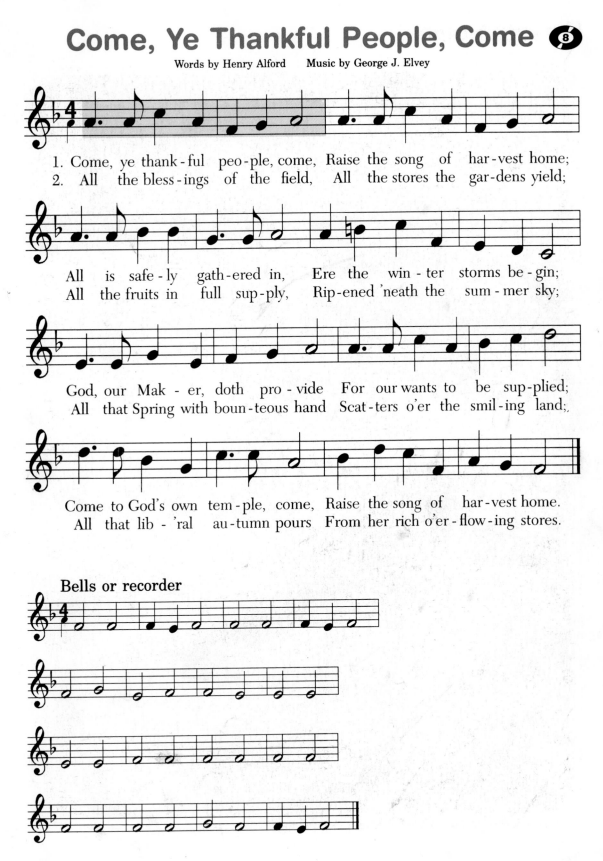

1. Come, ye thank-ful peo-ple, come, Raise the song of har-vest home;
2. All the bless-ings of the field, All the stores the gar-dens yield;

All is safe-ly gath-ered in, Ere the win-ter storms be-gin;
All the fruits in full sup-ply, Rip-ened 'neath the sum-mer sky;

God, our Mak-er, doth pro-vide For our wants to be sup-plied;
All that Spring with boun-teous hand Scat-ters o'er the smil-ing land;

Come to God's own tem-ple, come, Raise the song of har-vest home.
All that lib-'ral au-tumn pours From her rich o'er-flow-ing stores.

**Bells or recorder**

# A Hymn of Praise

Listen to the recording of this song. Can you name the instrument that accompanies the voices?

## For the Beauty of the Earth

Words by Folliott S. Pierpoint    Music Arranged from Conrad Kocher

1. For   the __ beau - ty   of   the   earth,

For   the   beau - ty   of   the   skies,

For   the __ love   which   from   our   birth

O - ver   and   a - round   us   lies,

Lord   of   all,   to   Thee   we   raise

This   our   hymn   of   grate - ful   praise.

2. For the beauty of each hour
   Of the day and of the night,
   Hill and vale and tree and flower,
   Sun and moon and stars of light, . . . .

# Swahili Prayer

## 'Sante-sana

Words and Music by Linda Williams

1. 'San - te    sa - na, __ Lord,   for   the   morn - ing, __
2. 'San - te    sa - na, __ Lord,   for   the   hunt - ers, __

'San - te    sa - na, __ Lord,   for   the   light,
'San - te    sa - na, __ Lord,   for   their   might,

For   the   bird  that  sings,  For   the   joy   it  brings;
Guide them   as   they roam,  Bring them   safe - ly  home,

'San - te    sa - na, __ Thank   you    Lord.
'San - te    sa - na, __ Thank   you    Lord.

3.  For the cattle safe from the lion,
    For the village safe in your sight,
    For the fields of grain,
    Blessed with sun and rain,
    'Sante-sana, Thank you Lord.

4.  Bless my brothers, Lord, and my sisters,
    Bless our slumber, Lord, through the night,
    Bring another day,
    Hear us when we pray,
    'Sante-sana, Thank you Lord.

© 1986 SUNDANCE MUSIC

# A Song for Winter

In some parts of our country, wintertime is snow time.
What kind of things do you do out of doors in wintertime?

## Winter Wonderland ⑧

Words by Dick Smith      Music by Felix Bernard

Sleigh-bells ring,    are you lis - t'nin'?
Gone a - way    is the blue - bird

In the lane    snow is glis - t'nin',
Here to stay    is a new bird,

A beau - ti - ful sight, _ We're hap - py to - night, _
He's sing - ing a song _ as we go a - long, _

**1.** Walk - in' in   a win - ter won - der land!    **2.** land!

© 1934 (Renewed) WB Music Corp. All Rights Reserved. Used by permission.

In the mead - ow we can build a snow - man,

And pre - tend that he's a cir - cus clown;

We'll have lots of fun with Mis - ter Snow - man

Un - til the oth - er kid - dies knock 'im down!

When it snows, ain't it thrill - in'?

Tho' your nose gets a chill - in',

We'll frol - ic and play _ the Es - ki - mo way, _

Walk - in' in a win - ter won - der land!

# Spin the Dreydl

Some children celebrate Chanukah with games and songs. The game Spin the Dreydl, though hundreds of years old, is still popular today.

Listen for the tambourine pattern in the recording of this song. Then find the pattern in the color box.

## Dreydl Song ⑧

Folk Song from Israel    English Words by Rosemary Jacques

Cha - nu - kah,    days    of    joy,

Hap - py    time _ for _ girls   and   boys;

Glow - ing    lights,    joy - ous    sounds,

Drey - dl   spin - ning    round   and   round.

It    re - minds   us    of    the    glo - ry

From: NOW WE BEGIN by Marian J. and Efraim M. Rosenzweig. Used by permission of Union of American Hebrew Congregations.

Of the days of Ju - dah Mac - ca - bee;

Spin the drey - dl, tell the sto - ry

Oh, what fun for you and me.

# Festival of Light

Show that you hear the two sections of this song. Tap the steady beat during section A. Clap the steady beat during section B.

## Make a Little Music for Chanukah

Words and Music by David Eddleman

1. When the chill is in the air and nights are get-ting long,
2. Now the can-dles all are burn-ing, burn-ing, oh, so bright,

Peo-ple light their can-dles and they sing a hap-py song
Fill-ing ev-'ry hap-py heart with warm and cheer-ful light,

A-bout a He-brew he-ro and a lan-tern burn-ing bright,
Tell-ing us that once there was a mir-a-cle, they say,

Then you know you must get read-y for the Fes-ti-val of Light.
When the lan-tern burned for eight long nights with oil for but one day.

Copyright © 1981 Coronet Press. Used by permission

**B**

E MIN

Make a lit-tle mu - sic, make a lit-tle mu - sic,

E MIN        D        E MIN

Make a lit-tle mu - sic for Cha - nu - kah;

E

Make a lit-tle mu - sic, make a lit-tle mu - sic,

E MIN        D        E MIN

Make a lit-tle mu - sic for Cha - nu - kah.

## Patterns for Percussion

Play these patterns with section A.

Finger Cymbals

Tambourine

Play these patterns with section B.

Finger Cymbals

Tambourine

## December

I like days
with a snow-white collar,
and nights when the moon
is a silver dollar,
and hills are filled
with eiderdown stuffing
and your breath makes smoke
like an engine puffing.

I like days
when feathers are snowing,
and all the eaves
have petticoats showing,
and the air is cold,
and the wires are humming,
but you feel all warm . . .
with Christmas coming!

*Aileen Fisher*

## A Song for Christmas

Follow along in your book as you listen to this merry Christmas song. Sing along when you can.

# Merry, Merry Christmas 
Traditional

Mer - ry, mer - ry Christ - mas ev - 'ry - where,

Cheer - i - ly it rings out through the air.

Christ - mas bells, Christ - mas trees, Christ - mas car - ols on the breeze.

Mer - ry, mer - ry Christ - mas ev - 'ry - where,

Cheer - i - ly it rings out on the air.

Why should we so joy - ous be, On this Christ - mas morn - ing?

An - gels sang in Beth - le - hem, On this Christ - mas morn - ing.

From *Adventures in Singing* Copyright © 1953 by Birch Tree Group, Ltd. All rights reserved. Used by permission.

# Christmas Bells

I heard the bells on Christmas day
Their old familiar carols play,
And wild and sweet the words repeat
Of peace on earth, good will to men.

# Christmas Is Coming

Polish Folk Tune        Words by Helen Bonney Kilduff

1. Christ - mas is com - ing; Oh, the hap - py day!
2. Christ - mas bells ring - ing On the frost - y air,

Christ - mas is com - ing, Sing a roun - de - lay.
Glad voic - es sing - ing, Joy is ev - 'ry - where.

Through the air gay tunes are ring - ing: Can it be the
Peace on earth, good - will they're bring - ing, Let us come and

an - gels sing - ing On this hap - py day?
join the sing - ing; Christ - mas Day is here!

From *Adventures in Singing* Copyright © 1953 by Birch Tree Group, Ltd. All rights reserved. Used by permission.

# A Swedish Christmas Song

In Sweden, children sing this song as they dance around the Christmas tree.

## Christmas Is Here Again

Swedish Folk Song

Christ-mas is here a-gain, Oh, Christ-mas is here a-gain,

Our hol-i-days will last till Eas-ter.

Then it is Eas-ter-time, Oh, then it is Eas-ter-time,

And Eas-ter joy will last till Christ-mas.

Words copyright 1934, 1961 G. Schirmer, Inc. Reprinted by permission.

## Countermelody for Bells

# Christmas Song from Mexico

To children in Mexico, Christmas Eve is an exciting time.

## Piñata 🎱8

Christmas Song from Mexico    English Words by Nona K. Duffy

Bril-liant lan-terns are light-ed, Our friends are in-vit-ed,

In cho-rus u-nit-ed, "¡Pi - ña - ta!"

There's no need to re-mind us, With blind-folds they'll bind us,

They'll turn and they'll wind us, "¡Pi - ña-ta!"

The *pi - ña - ta,* the *pi - ña - ta,*

Holds the can-dies for neigh-bors and cous-ins;

We will whack it, we will crack it,

And the good-ies will fall down in doz-ens.

All the chil-dren will scram-ble for can-dy,

All the chil-dren will scram-ble and shout;

All the chil-dren will grab for a cook-ie

And the oth-er good things that spill out.

# A Christmas Lullaby

How do you think this song should be sung? The headline at the top of the page will give you a hint.

## The Rocking Carol

Mexican Christmas Carol

A la ru - ru - ru, my ba - by dear - est,

Oh, sleep, my ba - by, oh, sleep, my fair - est. _____

The cat - tle now have ceased their gen - tle low - ing,

The si - lence of the beasts, de - vo - tion show - ing.

A la ru - ru - ru, my ba - by dear - est,

Oh, sleep, my ba - by, oh, sleep, my fair - est. _____

© 1952 Oliver Ditson Company. Reproduced by permission of the publisher Theodore Presser Company

On this recording you will hear another Christmas lullaby played by brass instruments. If you know the tune, hum along.

 *Coventry Carol*........**Old English Melody**

*Gypsy Woman with Baby; Amedeo MODIGLIANI; National Gallery of Art, Washington; Chester Dale Collection.*

**GYPSY WOMAN WITH BABY**
**AMEDEO MODIGLIANI**

## Sing with Joy

Try not to get lost in this add-on song. Follow the words as you listen to the recording. Join in when you can.

# Children, Go Where I Send Thee

American Folk Song

1. Chil-dren, go where I send thee; How shall I send thee?

I will send thee one by one. __

Well, one was the lit-tle bit-ty ba - by, __

Wrapped in swad-dling cloth - ing, __

Ly-ing in the man - ger. __

Born, born, _ oh, __ Born in Beth-le-hem. __

214

2. Children, go where I send thee;
How shall I send thee?
I will send thee two by two.
Well, two was the Paul and Silas,
One was the little bitty baby,
Wrapped in swaddling clothing,
Lying in the manger.
Born, born, oh,
Born in Bethlehem.

3. . . . I will send thee three by three.
Well, three was the three men riding,
Two was the Paul and Silas, . . .

4. . . . I will send thee four by four.
Well, four was the four come a-knocking at the door,
Three was the three men riding, . . .

5. . . . I will send thee five by five.
Well, five was the Gospel preachers,
Four was the four come a-knocking at the door, . . .

6. . . . I will send thee six by six.
Well, six was the six that couldn't be fixed,
Five was the Gospel preachers, . . .

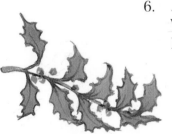

7. . . . I will send thee seven by seven.
Well, seven was the seven who went to heaven,
Six was the six that couldn't be fixed, . . .

8. . . . I will send thee eight by eight.
Well, eight was the eight who stood by the gate,
Seven was the seven who went to heaven, . . .

9. . . . I will send thee nine by nine.
Well, nine was the nine who saw the sign,
Eight was the eight who stood by the gate, . . .

10. . . . I will send thee ten by ten.
Well, ten was the Ten Commandments,
Nine was the nine who saw the sign, . . .

# A New Year's Carol

At New Year's time, children in Canada go from house to house to visit their neighbors. "Mistletoe Gifts" is one of the children's favorite songs.

## Mistletoe Gifts 9

French-Canadian Carol

1. Luck to the mas - ter and the mis - tress,
2. Gifts for the New Year will be wel - come,

Luck to the peo - ple dwell - ing here,
Wel - come to us and luck to you,

Wheth - er a cot - tage or a cas - tle,
He who be - stows a New Year to - ken,

Luck to you all and good New Year!
Shall have good luck the whole year through.

**REFRAIN**

If we __ please you with our sing - ing,

Sing - ing loud and clear,

Out of the cup-board gifts be bring-ing,

Gifts to give us cheer,

Luck to the mas - ter and the mis - tress,

Luck to you all and good New Year!

## Old Father Time

Old Father Time on New Year's Day
  Picked up his bag of months and years.
Thrust in his hand in a careless way,
  And pulled a wee fellow out by the ears.

"There you are," said he to the waiting crowd,
  "He's as good as any I have in my pack.
I never can tell, but I hope to be proud
  Of the little rascal when I come back."

*Leroy F. Jackson*

# Ribbons and Lace

Can you make a valentine? The words of this song tell you how.

## It's For My Valentine ⑨

Words and Music by Linda Williams

1. I think I'll start with a pa - per heart,
   leave some space for a bit of lace,
   if there's time, I'll in - vent a rhyme,

and I'll paint some flow - ers on it.
and I'll tie a rib - bon on it.
may - be e - ven write a son - net,

I'll make it all in my own de - sign,
And when it's done it'll ___ look so fine!
Or some - thing sim - ple like "Please be mine."

**1.,2.**

It's for my val - en - tine.      2. I'll
It's for my val - en - tine.      3. And
It's for my val - en -

**3.**

*slower*

tine.      Won't you be my val - en - tine?

© 1986 SUNDANCE MUSIC

Use this bell part to introduce the singing.

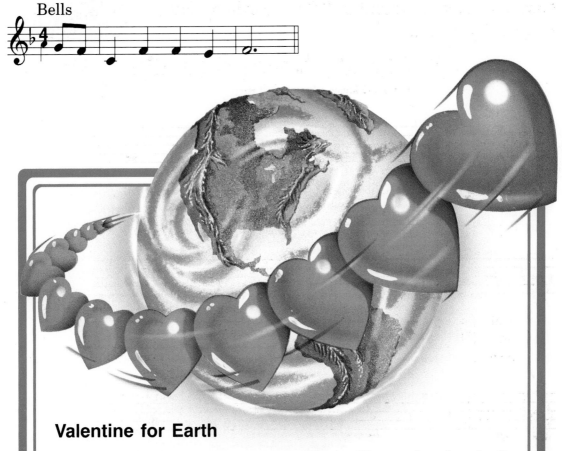

**Bells**

## Valentine for Earth

Oh, it will be fine
To rocket through space
And see the reverse
Of the moon's dark face,

To travel to Saturn
Or Venus or Mars,
Or maybe discover
Some uncharted stars.

But do they have anything
Better than we?
Do you think, for instance,
They have a blue sea

For sailing and swimming?
Do planets have hills
With raspberry thickets
Where a song sparrow fills

The summer with music?
And do they have snow
To silver the roads
Where the school buses go?

Oh, I'm all for rockets
And worlds cold or hot,
But I'm wild in love
With the planet we've got!

*Frances M. Frost*

## A Funny Valentine

How many times do you find this pattern in the song?

# Never Gonna Be Your Valentine

Words and Music by Linda Williams

1. I don't wan-na be your val - en - tine,
2. I'm not gon-na be your val - en - tine,

I don't wan-na be your val - en - tine,
I'm not gon-na be your val - en - tine,

Don't wan-na be your val - en - tine to - day!
You're not the kind of val - en - tine I like!

Oh, no, I don't wan-na be your val - en - tine,
Oh, no, I'm not gon-na be your val - en - tine,

I don't wan-na be your val - en - tine,
I'm not gon-na be your val - en - tine,

© 1986 SUNDANCE MUSIC

220

Pack up your val - en - tine and go a - way!
Pack up your val - en - tine and take a hike!

You nev - er let me win at games,
You won't share this, you won't lend that.

You laugh at me and call me names,
Won't e - ven let me pet your cat!

So e - ven if you beg and plead and whine, _____
And yet you bor - row ev - 'ry - thing that's mine! _____

I'm nev - er gon-na be your val - en - tine! _____
I'm nev - er gon-na be your val - en - tine!

3.  I might wanna be your valentine,
I might wanna be your valentine,
Don't tell a soul, 'cause you know very well
If all my friends knew I was your valentine,
They'd tease me and call me "Valentine,"
That's why you have to promise not to tell!
But you're so mean, you won't keep still!
You'll tell them all, I know you will!
So even though I think you're really fine,
I'm never gonna be your valentine!

# Can You Read This?

You know this is music. Do you know how it sounds?

Can you read this?

Oh, give me a home
Where the buffalo roam,
Where the deer and the antelope play . . .

You can read words. You have learned that the
letters tell you what the words sound like.

You can begin to read music when you learn how
music is written down. The written music tells you
how the music sounds.

You can read the rhythm of music.
Clap this pattern of even notes:

Here is a rhythm pattern with some short notes and
some longer ones. Clap this new pattern:

You can read rhythm patterns. Clap this mixed
up pattern. You can clap along with a song from
your book.

You have been clapping rhythm patterns in four.
Clap this pattern in three.

Here is a pattern in two.

When you add the *staff* you can tell if the melody of
the music moves up in pitch, moves down, or stays
on the same note.

You can read the rhythm of the music, and you can
read the direction of the melody.

Here are some melodies to read and sing. You can sing them with a song in your book.

This is a very short melody. You can sing it over and over to make a countermelody. This kind of countermelody is called an *ostinato*.

Here is another ostinato. Both of these melodies move *by step*. Each note is just next door to the other notes around it.

This ostinato moves *by leap*. It jumps over the next-door notes and lands on notes that are further away.

Here is a longer melody. Sometimes it moves by step, and sometimes by leap!

So far, you have been reading and singing melodies in rhythm patterns of two or four. Here is a melody you will count in three.

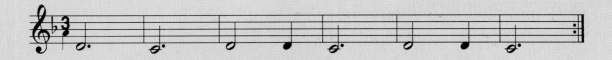

This melody uses a rhythm pattern that is uneven. Some *dotted notes* are next to short notes, making the rhythm "hop" in a dotted-note pattern.

Here is a countermelody for you to read and sing that will fit with *two* different songs in your book!

# Playing the Recorder

Using your left hand, cover the holes shown in the first diagram.

Cover the tip of the mouthpiece with your lips. Blow gently as you whisper "daah." You will be playing *B*.

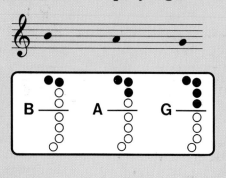

When you can play B, A, and G, you will be able to play melody 1.

1.

B A G

Practice playing two new notes—high C and high D. When you can play them, you are ready to try melody 2 at the top of the next page.

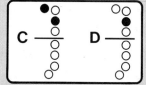

C      D

2.

D     C B     A G

Here are four new notes to practice. When you can play them, you will be ready to try melody 3.

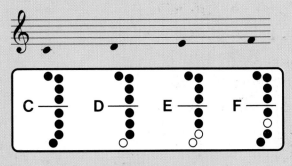

3.

E D C

Using the notes you have learned so far, you will be able to play some songs in your book. Try one of these.
- H'Atira, page 12
- Alekoki, page 64
- Scotland's Burning, page 111
- The Jasmine Flower, page 158

Here are two new notes to practice—F♯ and B♭. When you can play them, you will be ready to try one of the songs listed below.
- The Little Bells of Westminster, page 62
- Little Boy of the Sheep, page 145
- Lovely Evening, page 63
- Brother John, page 107

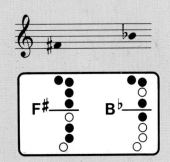

# The Sound Bank

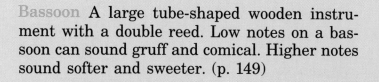

**Bassoon** A large tube-shaped wooden instrument with a double reed. Low notes on a bassoon can sound gruff and comical. Higher notes sound softer and sweeter. (p. 149)

**Clarinet** An instrument shaped like a long cylinder. It is usually made of wood and has a reed in the mouthpiece. The clarinet's low notes are soft and hollow. The highest notes are thin and piercing. (p. 127)

**Flute** A small metal instrument shaped like a pipe. The player holds the flute sideways and blows across an open mouthpiece. The flute's voice is clear and sweet. (p. 127)

**French Horn** A medium-sized instrument made of coiled brass tubing. At one end is a large "bell," at the other end a mouthpiece. The sound of the horn is mellow and warm. (p. 106)

**Guitar** A string instrument plucked with the fingers or a pick. A guitar can play a melody. It can also make chords to accompany a melody. Electric guitars sound much louder than a regular guitar. They can also make many special sounds. (p. 121)

**Harpsichord** A keyboard instrument shaped something like a piano. When the keys are pressed, the strings inside the instrument are plucked by small quills. This gives the sound a tinkling quality. (p. 164)

Oboe A slender wooden instrument with a double reed. In its low voice, the oboe can sound mysterious. When it goes higher, the sound is thin and sweet.

Piano A large keyboard instrument with strings inside. When the keys are pressed, hammers inside the piano hit the strings. The piano can play very high and very low sounds; very soft and very loud sounds. (p. 100)

Recorder A simple wooden instrument. It has a "whistle" mouthpiece at one end and holes in the side that can be covered and uncovered to change pitches. The recorder comes in various sizes, the larger ones sounding lower, the smaller ones higher. (p. 126)

Trombone A fairly large brass instrument with a large "bell" at the end of the tubing and a long curved "slide." The trombone can be loud and brilliant, but its soft voice is mellow. (p. 127)

Trumpet A small brass instrument with a "bell" at the end of its coiled tubing. The trumpet's voice can be loud and bright, but can also sound warm and sweet. (p. 127)

Tuba A very large brass instrument with a wide "bell" at the end of coiled tubing. The tuba's low notes are soft and dark-sounding. The higher ones are full and warm. (p. 106)

# Glossary

AB form (p. 116) A musical plan that has two different parts, or sections.

ABA form (p. 118) A musical plan that has three sections. The first and last sections are the same. The middle section is different.

accompaniment (p. 33) Music that supports the sound of the featured performers.

ballad (p. 156) In music, a song that tells a story.

chord (p. 106) Three or more different tones played or sung together.

composer (p. 24) A person who makes up pieces by putting sounds together in his or her own way.

contrast (p. 121) Two or more things that are different. In music, slow is a contrast to fast; section A is a contrast to section B.

countermelody (p. 112) A melody that is played or sung at the same time as another melody.

dynamics (p. 145) The loudness and softness of sound.

form (p. 116) The overall plan of a piece of music.

harmony (p. 106) Two or more different tones sounding at the same time.

introduction (p. 62) In a song, music played before the singing begins.

leap (p. 98) To move from one tone to another, skipping over the tones in between.

lullaby (p. 66) A quiet song, often sung when rocking a child to sleep.

melody (p. 106) A line of single tones that move upward, downward, or repeat.

**melody pattern** (p. 35) An arrangement of pitches into a small grouping, usually occurring often in a piece.

**meter** (p. 82) The way the beats of music are grouped, often in sets of two or in sets of three.

**mood** (p. 100) The feeling that a piece of music gives. The *mood* of a lullaby is quiet and gentle.

**notes** (p. 91) Symbols for sound in music.

**ostinato** (p. 107) A rhythm or melody pattern that repeats.

**partner songs** (p. 108) Two or more different songs that can be sung at the same time to create harmony.

**phrase** (p. 51) A musical "sentence." Each *phrase* expresses one thought.

**refrain** (p. 32) The part of a song that repeats, using the same melody and words.

**repeated tones** (p. 92) Two or more tones in a row that have the same sound.

**repetition** (p. 121) Music that is the same, or almost the same, as music that was heard earlier.

**rests** (p. 91) Symbols for silences in music.

**rhythm pattern** (p. 117) A group of long and short sounds.

**round** (p. 110) A follow-the-leader process in which all sing the same melody but start at different times.

**shanties** (p. 26) Sailors' work songs.

**steady beat** (p. 7) Regular pulses.

**strong beat** (p. 87) The first beat in a measure.

**tempo** (p. 74) The speed of the beat in music.

**theme** (p. 25) An important melody that occurs several times in a piece of music.

**tone color** (p. 124) The special sound that makes one instrument or voice sound different from another.

# Classified Index

# Song Index

**236  Reference Bank**

# Acknowledgments

Credit and appreciation are due publishers and copyright owners for use of the following.

"Autumn Woods" from A WORLD TO KNOW by James S. Tippett. © 1933 by Harper & Brothers.

"Clipper Ships and Captains" from A BOOK FOR AMERICANS by Rosemary and Stephen Vincent Benet, Holt, Rinehart & Winston, Inc. Copyright, 1933, Rosemary and Stephen Vincent Benet. Copyright renewed © 1961 by Rosemary Carr Benet. Reprinted by permission of Brandt & Brandt Literary Agents, Inc.

"December" from TIRRA LIRRA by Laura E. Richards. Copyright 1932 by Laura E. Richards. Copyright renewed 1960 by Hamilton Richards. Used by permission of Little, Brown & Company.

"Eletelephony" from TIRRA LIRRA by Laura E. Richards. © 1918 by Laura E. Richards. By permission of Little, Brown & Company.

"Far As Man Can See" from THE INDIANS BOOK by Natalie Curtis. Published by Dover Publications. Used by permission.

"Fireworks" by James Reeves. © James Reeves Estate. Reprinted by permission of the James Reeves Estate.

"Hallowe'en Indignation Meeting" from POEMS MADE TO TAKE OUT, © 1963, Margaret Fishback. Published by David McKay Company, Inc.

"In Beauty Happily I Walk" Courtesy American Museum of Natural History.

"A Modern Dragon" By Rowena Bastin Bennett. Reprinted by permission of the Estate of Rowena Bastin Bennett.

"Old Father Annum" from THE PETER PATTER BOOK by Leroy F. Jackson. Reprinted by permission of MacMillan Publishing Company.

"Open Range" from COWBOYS AND INDIANS by Kathryn and Byron Jackson. © 1968, 1948 Western Publishing Company, Inc. Used by permission.

"Valentine for Earth" from THE LITTLE NATURALIST by Frances M. Frost. Copyright 1959 by the Estate of Frances M. Frost. Published by Whittlesey House. Used by permission of McGraw-Hill Book Company, Inc.

The editors of Silver Burdett & Ginn Inc. have made every attempt to verify the source of "The Tired Scarecrow" and "Mistletoe Gifts," but were unable to do so. We believe them to be in public domain.

# Picture Credits

**Contributing Artists:**   Bill Bell; Christopher Calle; Lee Gaskins III; Ketti Kupper; Barbara Lanza; Don Patterson; Steve Schindler; George Vaquero; Chuck Wimmer.

**Photographs:**   All photographs by Silver Burdett & Ginn (SB&G) unless otherwise noted.

20: Scott Ransom/Taurus Photos. 21: Barney Nelson/Black Star. 24: Eric Reiner/Shostal Associates. 32–33: The Bettmann Archive. 39: Tommy Wadelton/Shostal Associates. 56: Dan DeWilde for SB&G. 61: Art Resource. 64: Errol de Silva/Camera Hawaii. 74: *t.* Chuck Muhlstock/Black Star; *b.* Richard Howard/Black Star. 76: *l.* Chuck Muhlstock/Black Star; *r.* John Launois/Black Star. 103: F.D. Peele/Berg & Associates. 108–109: Imagery for SB&G. 116: Dan DeWilde for SB&G. 124: *m.* Imagery for SB&G. 126: Victoria Beller-Smith for SB&G. 127: *t.l., b.r.* John Bacchus for SB&G. 128: © 1983 Martha Swope. 148: © 1985 Martha Swope. 151: H. Lanks/Shostal Associates. 190: © Jim Goodwin/Photo Researchers, Inc. 196: © Earl Roberge/Photo Researchers, Inc. 210: Imagery for SB&G.

Sound Bank Photographs: SB&G and John Bacchus, courtesy of Dorn & Kirschner Band Instrument Co., Union, N.J. and Yamaha International Corporation, Buena Park, Ca.

3 4 5 6 7 8 9 10—RRD—95 94 93 92 91 90 89 88

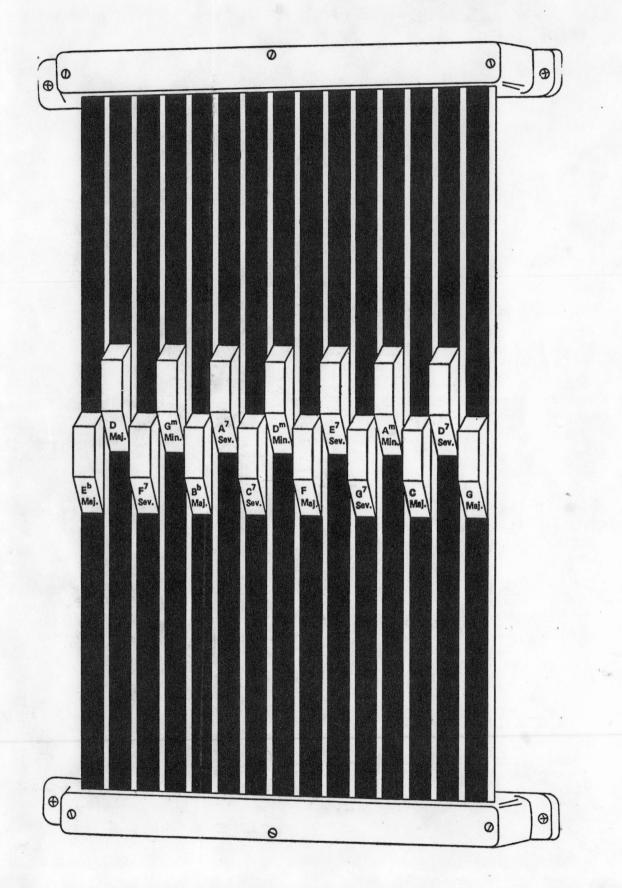